RESCUE DOGS

Where They Come From,
Why They Act the Way They Do,
and How to Love Them Well

PETE PAXTON

with

GENE STONE

A TarcherPerigee Book

tarcher
perigee

an imprint of Penguin Random House LLC
penguinrandomhouse.com

Most TarcherPerigee books are available at special quantity discounts for bulk purchase for sales
promotions, premiums, fund-raising, and educational needs. Special books or book excerpts also can
be created to fit specific needs. For details, write: SpecialMarkets@penguinrandomhouse.com.

LIBRARY OF CONGRESS CATALOGING-IN-PUBLICATION DATA
Names: Paxton, Pete, author.
Title: Rescue dogs : where they come from, why they act the way they do,
and how to love them well / Pete Paxton with Gene Stone.
Description: New York : TarcherPerigee, [2019] | Includes index.
Identifiers: LCCN 2019021678 | ISBN 9780525540359 (hardcover) |
ISBN 9780525540373 (ebook)
Subjects: LCSH: Rescue dogs.
Classification: LCC SF428.55 .P39 2019 | DDC 636.7/0886—dc23
LC record available at https://lccn.loc.gov/2019021678
p.   cm.

Printed in the United States of America
1   3   5   7   9   10   8   6   4   2

Book design by Nancy Resnick

Some names and identifying characteristics have been changed
to protect the privacy of the individuals involved.

For everyone defending those who cannot defend themselves

RESCUE DOGS

Praise for *Rescue Dogs*

"*Rescue Dogs* gives voice to the thousands of animals waiting in shelters across the country for adoption, and the thousands more who suffer and die to supply pet stores. Yet for all he has witnessed, Pete Paxton never loses empathy for the people who have failed these animals. This may be the biggest contributor to his success as an investigator and an advocate."

> —Scott Howe, Executive Director and CEO, Animal Rescue Fund of the Hamptons

"Pete Paxton is truly a hero, and in this game-changing new book, you can learn from him how to be one, too. This heartbreaking, and heartwarming, manifesto not only provides first-hand undercover accounts of the hidden horrors that too many dogs undergo, but at the same time, it walks you through everything you need to know to turn your own rescue dog's life around. A hugely important read for anyone who cares about dogs."

> —Mariann Sullivan, cofounder of Our Hen House and host of *The Animal Law* podcast

"*Rescue Dogs* is a must-read for any dog lover. Stories of truth, heartbreak, and triumph are detailed in a way that reflects the puppy mill and breeding industry, educating people who may not know the realities of these places otherwise. *Rescue Dogs* gives the average dog lover true insight into the realities that some dogs face and animal welfare workers learn."

> —Katera Berent, communications and events manager, Austin Pets Alive!

"Pete Paxton is an American hero: He has done more good work for dogs than anyone could possibly imagine. Inside this book are the extraordinary tales of his gripping adventures in the underbelly of the canine world, and then sound advice on what to do once you decide that you need to bring a rescue dog home. If you love dogs, you will absolutely love this book."

> —Rip Esselstyn, founder of Engine 2 and host of the *Plant-Strong* podcast

"What is a rescue dog? And who does the rescuing? Pete Paxton and Gene Stone's book explains it all through moving stories of dogs and their people, the work done by animal organizations both large and small, and how each of us can play a part. *Rescue Dogs* is the perfect primer for anyone interested in the work of rehoming pets and the joy brought by dogs who help us define what it means to have a home."   —Ken Foster, bestselling author of *The Dogs Who Found Me*

"I don't know the last time I've read a book as important as this one—you will leave this wonderfully well-written, totally engaging book with a powerful understanding about the way dogs are treated in this country—and what you can do about it. Highly recommended!"
 —Kathy Freston, *New York Times*–bestselling author and wellness activist

"What an extraordinary and important book this is—it's gripping and heartwarming, informative and entertaining. And I suspect it's impossible to read without wanting to go out and rescue a dog—or two!"   —Gene Baur, president and cofounder of Farm Sanctuary

"Thanks to undercover investigators like Pete, many more people now understand that despite the deceptive advertising in stores and on websites, puppies sold in pet stores and online usually come from puppy mills, where dogs are raised in miserable conditions solely to churn out puppies for an unsuspecting public. Pete's tips on how to adopt a rescue dog and his advice for budding advocates will help inspire dog lovers to become part of the change until no more puppies are sold in pet stores and no more homeless dogs go without a family."
—Kathleen Summers, director of outreach and research for the Humane Society of the United States' puppy mill campaign

"Before you get a dog, buy this fascinating, beautifully written book that's both an adventure story and a how-to. Once you've read it, you will probably want to go right out and rescue a dog—and two lives will be forever changed."
—David Coman-Hidy, president of the Humane League

Contents

CONTENTS

PART III: HELPING RESCUES BEYOND YOUR HOME

INTRODUCTION

My name is Pete. I'm an undercover animal investigator.

You could be forgiven for thinking that's something out of *Ace Ventura: Pet Detective*.

Rather, I investigate the places that few people have seen—or ever want to see. I've infiltrated puppy mills that churn out thousands of puppies per year, seedy brokers who hoard puppies and peddle them off to research labs, and massive pet store chains. For eighteen years I have crisscrossed the country, talking my way into jobs at some of the most horrific puppy mills to gather evidence for law enforcement. I've gone to great lengths to avoid detection. I've cut, dyed, and shaved my hair multiple times; grown a beard so thick my friends didn't recognize me; switched accents when conducting investigations; developed a habit of wearing only neutral-colored clothing so I'm not easily recognized in crowds; changed my driver's license up to three times a year; and legally changed my name three times as well (my real name actually isn't Pete). My work has been the subject of two HBO documentaries, a National Geographic documentary, and countless magazine articles and television interviews. Most important, I have helped thousands of abused dogs find loving homes.

Typical puppy mill dogs are confined without any mental stimulation and are treated as breeding machines to churn out dogs for pet stores and online sellers. Taken at the puppy mill of Clinton Michel in Long Lane, Missouri.

Much of my work against puppy mills is on behalf of a small nonprofit called the Companion Animal Protection Society (CAPS). CAPS is run by Deborah Howard, an ambitious, focused, and tenacious woman who has made fighting puppy mills her life's work. Deborah has a handful of employees and many volunteers. Collectively, their efforts support tougher regulations on dog breeders and on pet stores from selling puppies and kittens from breeders. CAPS posts evidence online that is easily found by the public, and it takes risks. It's the only nonprofit that consistently puts investigators' field notes on its website for the public to see, allowing for full transparency. You don't have to trust CAPS's claims with blind faith or dig through websites to verify them; you can see the footage for yourself.

I've made my career operating in a nebulous area of the law. My work involves lying to people and gaining employment under false pretenses. It involves secretly filming people and their actions. It means gaining the trust of others—some of them bad, some of them good—and then breaking it repeatedly. Cops have threatened to arrest me more times than I can count. I've sat in the back of police cars arguing with officers about their local trespassing and audio recording laws. Throughout all this time, Deborah and CAPS have stood by and supported me. We've shut down some of the worst offenders and galvanized public support to pass new statewide laws to protect dogs.

I put myself through the emotional, physical, and financial abuse for one simple reason: I love dogs. I love happy dogs and sad dogs. I love old dogs who take halting steps and look intently at the floor as they scuttle past; young puppies who spin in circles, unable to contain their excitement; and stoic hunters who go about their lives with a sense of duty and loving loyalty. I love them all, regardless of where they have come from, who owns them, or what problems they may have.

I especially love the shivering dogs who fear everyone they see. I relate to them more than I do to people. All too often, people think rescue dogs' tough backgrounds mean they come with incurable disorders and irreparable damage. But I've seen firsthand how dogs who are rescued from the most terrible conditions can overcome their dark days to become wonderful companions for humans. I firmly believe that with a little bit of help, the vast majority of rescue dogs prove to be loving, loyal, and safe companions.

I've rescued dogs from some of the worst places on earth. Some of these cases involved my going undercover for six months or longer and coordinating with local law enforcement, the media, and other activist groups. A successful rescue operation requires countless moving parts and hard work from dozens, if not hundreds, of people.

But sometimes a successful rescue can be achieved by one guy in a truck. This is the story of Daisy, my simplest rescue, but also one of the most meaningful to me.

I was several years into my career as an undercover investigator, with a number of major victories under my belt. But I was burned out after spending nearly all my time on the road. I decided to unwind for a few weeks, visiting my parents, who lived in a military town. There, every time local soldiers were deployed, dogs would be surrendered to shelters or abandoned on the streets. The local community rallied to provide temporary homes for these stray dogs or bring them to no-kill shelters. The roster included Buddy, a skinny chow mix covered in two hundred ticks; Sandy, a leggy, athletic dog who loved to run through the woods; Snowcap, a beautiful, gentle husky; and Charlie, a beagle adopted by my parents' next-door neighbor.

Then there was Daisy. I found Daisy on my way to a local motocross track. Stopped at a traffic light, I saw a skinny, slow-moving dog wandering through the intersection. I threw my truck into park, jumped out, and, despite the dog's attempt to escape my clutches, hugged her tightly to my chest. She just didn't have it in her to move fast. I placed a leash around her neck. She began to convulse and whine. As I picked her up and carried her across the road, I felt her shaking violently.

Once inside my truck, Daisy sat quietly, still shaking and cowering toward the passenger-side door. A shepherd mix with dirty, matted brown, black, and white fur, she had a long snout, ears that pointed straight up, and a bushy tail. She looked to be about seven years old. She was barely twenty-five pounds, but she should have weighed closer to forty. Her teeth, stained and brown, were worn down almost to the gums—a sign that she had been chewing on rope and had spent most of her days tied up.

Daisy was sick, and her frightened behavior would make her unadoptable. She would be killed immediately at a normal shelter, and

Daisy healed my parents and me when we grieved Scotty's passing. We knew Scotty never could be replaced, and we eventually learned that Daisy never could either.

all the no-kill shelters in the area were full. I turned my truck around and brought her to my parents' house. At the time our family dog, Scotty, was in very poor health. A nineteen-year-old cairn terrier, Scotty had lived the spoiled life. But now his heart was expanding, putting pressure on his lungs. Soon he would need to be put to sleep. My parents agreed to take Daisy in, but they made it clear they were not going to keep her once Scotty passed. They could never replace Scotty.

I named the little rescue Daisy. It was an optimistic name; I hoped this poor, pitiful creature would blossom into a dog who wasn't terrified of people. Although she did start to relax around me, she continued to shake uncontrollably around my father despite his affection toward her. In fact, whenever a strange man entered the home, Daisy would run to the back door, her eyes wild and body trembling. Yet Scotty loved having Daisy around. He would lie next to her, the two senior dogs enjoying each other's warm company. His body was slowly shutting down, but Daisy helped him be at peace for his final weeks of life.

One day Scotty couldn't get up, and we knew it was time. Daisy must have sensed what was happening, because she refused to leave his side. We took Scotty to the vet and stood next to him as he lay down calmly on the exam table. We petted and soothed him while he received one injection to render him unconscious and another to stop his heart. In silence, and with no movement other than his chest letting out one final breath, Scotty passed away.

At this point, Daisy, still a guest in my parents' home, hadn't yet adjusted. She still needed to be reassured that any man in the house wasn't going to beat her, that we were nearby, and that we weren't angry with her. My parents were devastated after Scotty's passing, but they were also used to having a fluffball to spoil. Now that Scotty was gone, my mother began counting on seeing Daisy bound joyfully through the yard while she was gardening. My dad loved coming home and petting Daisy on the head, watching as she gradually but surely realized he was a friend. But she was still a "temporary" dog.

After a few months, Daisy started barking at strangers who were strolling down the street. This meant she was feeling a part of our pack and that she had a role to play: guard dog. My parents' initial resolve not to keep Daisy faded. Daisy needed care and emotional support, but so did my parents. It turned out the only thing that could comfort us after Scotty died was another dog. Being able to heal Daisy was exactly what healed us.

I didn't rescue Daisy from a puppy mill or a research lab. Rescuing her didn't require hidden cameras, lawyers, the media, or the countless other moving parts that are necessary in my work. Daisy wasn't even the first dog I rescued, but in many ways she was the most important. Undercover animal investigations is not a lucrative job. I'm traveling constantly. I don't see my family enough. I have to lie repeatedly. I sometimes work beside dangerous people who would not appreciate being secretly recorded. Many of the law enforcement officials I work with are diligent and professional, but some are good old boys who view me as a threat. I see dogs hit, punched, and killed—and many times there is nothing I can do. I invest every ounce of energy into shutting down a puppy mill, then watch as another dozen pop up the following week.

All this takes a physical and emotional toll. But Daisy reminded me every day why I got involved in rescue work in the first place. By finding her forever home, she gave hope to the millions of strays, puppy mill dogs, and other rescues who are still searching for theirs. I've devoted my life to helping them.

This book is divided into three parts. In Part 1, I share the stories of eight individual dogs from my eighteen years of investigations. Although their stories are very different, they collectively paint a portrait of how dogs are bought and sold in America. Some of these stories have happy endings. Others do not. You'll meet Spot, the first dog I ever tried to rescue; Rebel, who was owned by one of the country's most notorious dog traffickers, a man who made his existence peddling dogs to research labs; the "perfect puppy," one of 86,000 nameless puppies who each year passed through the doors of the single largest broker of dogs in the country, where I worked for six months; Sugar, whom I rescued from an unsettling puppy mill operator turned exorcist; a white Pomeranian who taught me that sometimes the greatest obstacle for helping abused dogs is law enforcement itself; Davida, whose story helped lead to a landmark legislative victory for animal rights in Pennsylvania; an English bulldog named Maggie, whom I met working undercover at one of the most horrific puppy mills in history; and, finally, Emma, a very special Chihuahua whose story proves that even the most innocent-seeming kennels can harbor horrendous abuse.

Together, these stories point to a single conclusion: Your search for a dog should begin and end at your local animal shelter. Every year, 670,000 shelter dogs are euthanized, while approximately 2 million are purchased from stores and kennels. By purchasing a dog, no matter from where, you are contributing to the puppy mill industry.

If you are considering adopting a rescue dog, or if you recently have, Part 2 will guide you through everything you need to know. I draw on my firsthand experience to help you every step of the way, from choosing the right shelter to preparing your home and family for the unique needs of a rescue dog. Rescue dogs are special because they are survivors. They are hardy, strong, and infinitely adaptable. Rescues need to have navigated terrifying ordeals simply to have made it to a shelter. This may make them wary and suspicious of new environments, but it also means they learn and acclimate quickly. You'll learn about common rescue dog behavior, how to train rescues, and how to bond with them. Dogs rescued from puppy mills will respond to different methods than strays, who will respond different from owner surrenders. I've seen it all, and I believe that any dog can become a safe, loving, and loyal member of your family.

Throughout Part 2 you'll also read stories from people all over the world who decided to save a life and enrich their own forever.

But the rescue does not end at the shelter. You don't have to dedicate your life to working undercover to fight dog abuse, nor even adopt a dog. There's room for everyone in this fight. In Part 3, you'll read about ways to make life better for the rescues of tomorrow. This fight is winnable. For example, thanks to steady pressure by activists, California has effectively banned pet stores from selling non-rescued dogs. Pennsylvania, once considered the "puppy mill capital of the east," has passed two landmark laws that shut down nearly 75 percent of the state's puppy mills. Similar laws were passed in Missouri, a state notorious for being a hotbed of dog abuse, and its puppy mill population shrank from 2,000 to 809. While the diligent work of investigators helped spark these efforts, these laws never would have been possible without phone calls, letters, and petitions from people like you.

Dogs have walked steadfastly by our side for more than ten thousand years. Without them, the human race may not have survived. We have repaid this favor by tinkering with the extremes of genetics to produce dogs matching our fleeting needs. Our most loyal friends deserve better. This book is about my career, but it's also about the 3.3 million dogs who pass through shelters every year, desperate for a loving home. This is my story—and theirs.

PART I

RESCUE STORIES

SPOT

The Dog Who Changed My Life

I owe my career to a dog named Spot.

In 1998, I was volunteering for Habitat for Humanity in Fayette-ville, North Carolina, helping to repair homes for economically disadvantaged people. I was pursuing a career in law enforcement at the time. Police officers I'd greatly respected told me how much of their job was social work, so I was determined to begin meeting and helping people from very different backgrounds. Habitat for Humanity was the perfect way to do this.

After doing extensive repairs we always had leftover wood. My friend Ed Avent, who managed the Habitat volunteers, had met an old woman named Ms. Baker, who lived nearby and struggled to heat her home in the winter. He suggested we drop the extra wood at her house so she could burn it in her stove. The next day I threw the wood into my truck and drove over to Ms. Baker's house.

She lived at the end of a dirt road. The only buildings on it were her house and the church she attended. Her yard was a muddy patch of ground filled with weeds. Ms. Baker, in her eighties and very over-weight, struggled to move around on her own. She had a thick South-ern accent and managed to inject "the Lord" into nearly every sentence. Ms. Baker lived alone with a German shepherd–chow chow mix named Spot, a gorgeous dog with a flowing, lionlike mane, rounded black ears, and eyes that were playful and wild. He was only two or three years old, but Ms. Baker was struggling to take care of him. Spot lived outdoors in a dilapidated wooden doghouse. When I first saw him, he was nibbling on moldy biscuits and lapping up muddy sludge from his water bowl. His soaking-wet fur was caked in months-old mud, and he was tethered to the doghouse with a chain so mangled it was gouging his neck. He was at least fifteen pounds underweight.

I approached Ms. Baker while she sat in her porch rocking chair. "Ms. Baker," I said, "I can't help but notice that Spot isn't doing very well. He's so wet, and that chain is causing him to bleed."

"Mm-hmm," Ms. Baker replied. "Thank you for the firewood."

"If you don't mind, I'm going to start coming by and feeding him and changing his water. I'll also walk him and I'll keep bringing you firewood. Deal?" Ms. Baker huffed, harrumphed, and then agreed.

For the next few months I regularly visited Spot and Ms. Baker with an armload of firewood and a pocketful of kibble. At first Spot was just as skeptical of me as his owner was. He'd growl and nip at my hand when I gave him food; as he had never been trained, he hadn't learned to associate humans with care and shelter. Ms. Baker probably never petted him or let him inside the house, only occasionally tossing him scraps from her porch. Spot's entire life had been spent inside or next to that tiny doghouse. He had never learned to interact with another living thing and therefore was reverting to his most base instincts. When I stood next to him while he was eating, he thought I was threatening his catch. When I came over to pet him, he thought I was attacking.

For the first several weeks I tossed Spot his food from a distance, but I made sure he knew it was coming from me. After he had eaten,

I'd slowly approach, hold out my hand, and allow him to smell me for as long as he wanted. Sometimes he'd let me get close enough to attach a leash; other times he lunged at me and we'd have to try again the next day.

I had to learn to approach Spot calmly and confidently. If I acted with purpose, he was calmer. If I was hesitant, he would lash out. If I managed to coax him close to me, he'd let me pet and hold him for an hour. Once, while out for a walk, I came too close while Spot was sniffing a log and he lunged at me, barking and snapping. I retrieved a piece of baseboard from my truck and bound it to my jean jacket to protect my arm.

"Easy, Spot," I said. "Relax." I approached him again, and his ears were sticking back in submission. I waited until he calmed down and then brought him back to his doghouse. Spot was always calmer after he walked in the woods; he couldn't focus until he had burned off excess energy. If he wanted to go for another walk, we did that. If he wanted to slobber my face with kisses, we did that. Sometimes, all Spot wanted to do was sit with me and listen to the distant hum of traffic. We'd do that for hours at a time.

After several months Spot would come to me when I called him. He trusted me to refill his food dish. He patiently waited for me to slip the leash around his neck. He was gaining weight. When I pointed out how much better Spot was doing, Ms. Baker said, "Mm-hmm, thanks for the firewood."

I loved taking care of Spot, but I couldn't stay in Fayetteville forever. In the back of my mind, I knew the grim truth: As soon as I left, it would be back to the moldy biscuits, the muddy water bowl, the mangled chain. Spot wouldn't survive the winter.

"Ms. Baker," I pleaded. "Please let me take Spot. I can find him a good home."

She replied, "Nope. Thanks for the firewood."

I offered to bring her a year's supply of firewood. I offered to give her money for Spot. I all but fell onto my knees and begged, but she merely said: "Nope."

If I couldn't convince Ms. Baker to give up Spot, maybe someone else could. I knew she attended the church next door—what if I could speak to her pastor? Later that day I strolled over to the church, a medium-sized building nestled between two billboards on US 401. I wandered inside and found the church's manager. She was a kind-looking woman who listened intently as I explained the situation.

"I was hoping you or the pastor could speak with Ms. Baker about her dog, Spot," I said. "She really isn't able to care for him anymore and I'm worried he won't survive the cold weather."

"That is so kind of you to bring this to our attention," the woman replied. "Please follow me." *Finally*, I thought. *Now we're getting somewhere.* She walked me down a long corridor and opened a door leading back outside the building. "Out here, if you don't mind," the woman said. "This is such a noble concern you have."

I stepped outside and she slammed the door in my face.

Since I wasn't going to get much help from God on this one, I tried the next best thing: Cumberland County Animal Control. I spoke on the phone with a fellow who politely listened as I explained the situation once more.

"Is there any way we can compel Ms. Baker to give up her dog?" I asked him.

"I'm sorry, sir, there isn't anything we can do. You said yourself that she's feeding him and providing shelter."

"Moldy biscuits and a moldy doghouse with a hole in the roof."

The man sighed. "There's nothing we can do if you're also taking care of him."

It was a cruel catch-22: Animal control couldn't help because I was keeping Spot alive. If I wanted to save him, I'd have to leave him and therefore inflict pain.

"So if I leave him alone for a couple months, and his condition goes back to what it was, you can do something?" I asked, suppressing my anger.

"Possibly, but you'll need photographs. We'll need proof of neglect."

I visited Spot one more time. I snapped a few pictures as he padded over to me and licked my hands. I was still astounded by how he had transformed from a skin-and-bones rage machine to a bubbly poofball. All it had taken was gentle reinforcement and regular attention. When we went for a walk, Spot bounded proudly at my side. Gone were the days when I had to strap a wooden board to my arm for protection. Spot had come to rely on me not just for food but for attention and joy. I was the only source of happiness in his life, and it was breaking my heart to leave him at the mercy of a person who was not capable of caring for him.

I brought Ms. Baker one last load of firewood and said goodbye to Spot. He lay down next to his sad little doghouse and fell asleep. I drove off, hoping against hope he would still be alive in two months. My experience with Spot and Ms. Baker made me realize I enjoyed helping people. I wanted to do it for a living, so I soon enrolled in the local fire academy.

When I returned to Ms. Baker's home two months later, Spot was still alive—but only barely so. His fur was matted and covered in mud. His nails were overgrown. He had lost all the weight he had put on and then some. His muddy water bowl was leaking after he had nearly chewed through it. Spot was walking with a limp—his paw was caked with weeks-old blood. From a distance, he blended in with the muddy and feces-strewn ground he limped over. Spot looked at me with dim recognition, and he labored to his feet to say hello. He remembered.

"Hey, buddy," I said softly, snapping pictures of Spot's sorry state. "It's okay. It'll all be okay. I'll get you out of here." Later that day I hand-delivered the photos to Cumberland County Animal Control.

One of the officers agreed to pay Ms. Baker a visit. Encouraged, I began researching local shelters that could take Spot in. I even considered adopting Spot myself; he was such a special dog who deserved a loving home.

The next day I brought Ms. Baker another load of firewood. Spot greeted me like he always did, and I tossed him a biscuit. Then the house's screen door slammed. Ms. Baker was standing on her porch, leaning on a cane, glaring at me.

"Get the hell away from my dog and get off my property!" she yelled. "And don't you ever come back."

"Ma'am," I said, perplexed, "I'm just here to drop off wood and feed Spot, like always."

"You're here to steal my dog. The animal control people came by this morning and said you wanted them to take Spot away. I told them I never gave you permission to be on my property. Spot is my dog and I'll take care of him however I see fit."

"Ms. Baker," I pleaded, "I just want what's best for Spot. He is literally dying right now. How can you not see that?"

"He's fine, I'm fine, and I'm calling the cops. Don't ever come back on my property."

I begged Ms. Baker to let me take Spot. I appealed to her Christianity, desperately insisting that Jesus wouldn't want such a loving animal to starve to death. She refused. I appealed to her greed, saying I would buy him and she could use the money to buy a better stove. She refused. I appealed to her sense of morality, explaining that Spot was happiest with people who could walk and play with him. She refused. I made the final agonizing steps back to my truck, hoping Ms. Baker would change her mind. Spot wagged his tail as I walked by. I held out my hand as he limped over to give me a sloppy kiss. I gave him a biscuit and patted him on the head. Then I climbed into my truck and left.

I called Cumberland County Animal Control again, but it was

clear they weren't going to take action. In my experience, animal control almost never forcibly removes a companion animal from his or her owner unless neglect can be proven. Spot looked like crap, but Ms. Baker technically was providing food and water. And in a town of a hundred thousand people, there were too many strays, aggressive dogs, and wild animals the overburdened department needed to deal with. I was livid that they refused to help Spot, but there was nothing I could do.

That night the temperatures dipped into the teens, and I considered driving back to Ms. Baker's and taking Spot. To this day, when the temperature dips below freezing, I think about Spot shivering in his doghouse. But I didn't go back. I honored Ms. Baker's demands and I didn't return to her property. I left Fayetteville after deciding to change careers and headed to Harris County, Texas, to take a job working at Special Pals, a no-kill shelter.

More than a year later I was driving from Texas to my parents' home in North Carolina. The route brought me near Fayetteville. I had avoided thinking about Spot and Ms. Baker, but as I saw the exit signs for Fayetteville along I-95, I knew I had to know. Good or bad, I needed closure. I took the exit and drove along US 401, past the chapel, and up Ms. Baker's dirt driveway. There was Spot's yard, the same dilapidated doghouse. Except Spot wasn't there. In his place was a tiny, poofy, white Pomeranian puppy. She yipped at me as I peered at her. She was tied to a pole in the yard exactly in Spot's place. *Maybe Spot is hiding inside the doghouse*, I thought dimly. But he wasn't there.

Ms. Baker was sitting on her rocking chair. "Hi, Ms. Baker," I said. She nodded but didn't seem to recognize me.

"I used to bring you firewood and take care of Spot," I continued. "I see you have a new dog. Is Spot around?"

She sized me up briefly, then looked away into nothing. Then she said, flatly, "Gone."

I stared at her. I knew the answer before I asked, but hearing her say the word shook me to my core. I looked at the Pomeranian who had taken Spot's place. She was eating the same moldy kibble and drinking from the same muddy water bowl. I turned to say something, anything, to Ms. Baker, but no words came. I went back to my truck and left.

I made a decision later that night, one that would define the rest of my life. I wouldn't let what happened to Spot happen to the Pomeranian, and I wouldn't let it happen to any other abused dog I came across. This would mean upsetting dog owners. It would mean running afoul of law enforcement. I didn't care. If I had to drive back from Texas twice a month just to rescue dogs from Ms. Baker, I'd still do it. She could report me to the police. I didn't care. If saving this dog meant tacking a felony on to my record, so be it.

A few days later I retrieved an old dog crate at my parents' house and tossed it into the back of my truck. The weather report said that the temperature would be falling into the twenties—too cold for a months-old, malnourished Pomeranian. I gunned it down I-95, took the Fayetteville exit, and then tore past the church, my truck roaring as it flung up dust and gravel. I hurtled down Ms. Baker's driveway and stopped in front of her house. I kept the engine running in case I needed to make a fast getaway.

But the property was empty. The Pomeranian was gone. All that was left in her yard was the food bowl, the doghouse, and the mangled chain. Ms. Baker's rocking chair sat still on the porch, creaking slightly in the wind. I walked onto the porch and peered through the window. The house had been cleaned out.

I stopped by the church next door and inquired about Ms. Baker. She had died the previous week, a man told me. They didn't know what happened to the Pomeranian.

My experience with Spot set me on an unorthodox path. I learned that otherwise good people are capable of immoral actions when it comes to animals. Why wouldn't the local authorities simply enforce the law? Why wouldn't the local church want to help a neglected animal? Why wouldn't Ms. Baker give up a dog she imprisoned in a muddy yard? Against a community like that, saving dogs is very difficult. I'd learn this lesson again and again over my career. The entire community had to change. I needed to figure out how to go up against the system, not just individual people.

In the meantime I was taking classes at a local community college, but they were having little impact on me. Instead, volunteering to feed the homeless and working at animal shelters made me feel like I was growing as a person. As much as I respected law enforcement for being on the front lines of protecting the defenseless in society, I realized I wouldn't last long following orders that meant leaving dogs chained in front of moldy food.

I dropped out of college with no clear plan for my future. It sounded foolish and romantic, but the more I thought about it, the more I needed to do something meaningful for animals. I moved back to Houston to continue working with Special Pals. I learned to be a vet tech for dogs. I helped nurse sick and injured animals back to health and foster them until they were adopted. I joined the Houston Animal Rights Team, learning how to stage protests and educate the public about animal rights issues. I joined forces with an activist named Joe Feduccia, who was fighting pound seizure—a little-known practice in which local pounds sell dogs and cats for medical experimentation. Knowing that the public would be on my side if they were aware of it, I attended a county commissioner meeting to demand an end to the practice. Refusing to step down after my allotted three minutes were up, I was swiftly dragged out of the courtroom by police. Fortunately, local TV networks had filmed the altercation and broadcast it on the local news. After a month-long public uproar, Harris County officially ended the policy.

Being an activist was intoxicating. Even with limited resources, I could bring about meaningful change for dogs. But what about the other abuses that weren't making the local news? It had taken months of legwork for Joe to even find out about pound seizure. My stunt at the courtroom was merely the final stride in a marathon that involved scores of phone calls, surveillance, and investigative reporting. I enjoyed being on television, but I wanted to be like Joe. The real activist work meant turning video cameras away from my face and toward darker, more secret places.

I then arranged to meet a private investigator named Steve Garrett, who was working with a small activist group called Last Chance for Animals. Steve was unusual in the animal rights movement. He didn't think like traditional activists; he didn't socialize with them. He took one case at a time and devoted every waking hour to it. During our meeting he told me that he thought I could help him conduct mobile surveillance on brokers who were selling sick puppies to oblivious consumers. It was Steve who first suggested I try undercover investigations. This would mean learning to make myself forgettable. It would mean getting jobs in some of the worst places on earth. It would mean witnessing and standing by as people committed the kind of horrendous abuse toward animals that I wanted to stop. Except I wouldn't be sitting idly by. I would be waiting patiently like a fly on a wall—a fly with a video camera.

Sometimes I think back to that ramshackle house in the middle of North Carolina. I think about Ms. Baker and the church, but mostly I think about Spot. Even now, years later, I sometimes wonder what would have happened if I had simply taken Spot the moment I saw him.

In the end, I wasn't able to help Spot, but Spot was able to help me. He gave me purpose, and there is no greater gift.

REBEL

Undercover in the World of Research Dogs

O n a cold day in September 2001, I was trudging through the woods of rural Arkansas. My ankles burned as chiggers relentlessly bit into my skin. Walking beside me was Steve Garrett from Last Chance for Animals (LCA). We were trespassing on private property and armed with video cameras. We were here to shut down one of the most notorious dog traffickers in the country.

Our target was Martin Creek Kennels, operated by a man named CC Baird, who was responsible for peddling thousands of dogs each year to research labs. The use of dogs in research has long been controversial. The UK's National Anti-Vivisection Society estimates that approximately seventy thousand dogs are experimented on annually, with 75 percent of them used for pharmaceutical testing—despite many scientists concluding that dogs are poor predictors of drug effects in human bodies. Due to federal law, drug companies are required to test their products in both rodent and non-rodent experiments to gauge toxicity. Since dogs are docile and naturally trusting of humans, they make perfect test subjects.

Many lab dogs come from class A dealers, or licensed commercial breeders who sell purpose-bred dogs specifically for research. These animals, who are typically highly socialized beagles with known pedigrees, command a premium. Less picky laboratories often resort to class B dealers: licensed brokers who buy dogs from breeders and resell them to research labs or pet stores. These dogs are usually "random sourced," meaning their history is unknown. They could be strays. They could be owner surrenders. Or they could be stolen family pets.

CC Baird was the single largest class B dealer in the United States, and he was known to employ so-called bunchers to acquire his dogs in bulk, no questions asked. Legally, bunchers were only allowed to sell pets they personally owned. However, we suspected that Baird's bunchers were stealing pets. LCA also suspected Baird was acquiring dogs with heartworms—an ugly but easily treatable condition in which parasites infest dogs' hearts—and then killing the dogs to sell the worms to research labs. Steve and I were looking for a trench rumored to lay at the back of the property where Baird buried the dogs he had killed. If we could find evidence that these dogs were stolen or acquired illegally, we could bring down his operation.

After searching Baird's property for an hour, we finally found it: a giant trench more than a hundred feet long, six feet wide, and six feet deep. Everything was silent. Even the birds avoided this place. Next, the smell hit us: putrid, horrible decay. I suppressed the urge to vomit. We donned surgical masks and peered into the trench. Dead dogs, everywhere. Mosquitoes. Maggots. Skulls. Organs and guts splayed open. It was the most horrific scene I had ever encountered.

"Jump inside," Steve told me, handing me what looked like a small plastic radio. "Scan this near the dogs. It will beep if they have chip implants, and we'll know they were stolen."

I gazed at the muck below me. Steve sensed my hesitation and said, "Look, do you want to be an investigator or not? If you want to chain yourself to trees and scream at old ladies in fur coats, be my guest. But if you want to really do some good and help animals, get in that trench."

I took a deep breath and jumped in. The smell was overwhelming. I felt paralyzed in place.

"*Hurry up!*" Steve hissed, looking out for any kennel workers. It was broad daylight, and this being rural Arkansas, nearly everyone was armed.

I activated the scanner and waved it around the dead dogs. Everything was covered in blood. Dozens of surgical gloves lay around like discarded tissue paper. Steve continued to scan the trench.

"Over there," he said, gesturing at a stack of bloody papers. "What are those?"

I stepped over a heap of vials and needles and grabbed the papers, then stuffed them in my pocket.

"Grab whatever you can," Steve said. "Tags, needles, whatever—" He stopped midsentence. "*Oh shit.*"

Far off I heard a buzzing sound. I peeked over the trench and saw a cloud of dirt. It was an ATV coming directly for us. If we could see the driver, he could see us.

"Let's get the hell out of here," Steve yelled. "Take whatever you can."

I gathered up as much evidence as I could hold and scrambled out of the trench and made for tall grass. The ATV reached the trench just as we slipped into the woods. We broke into a sprint, dodging tree branches and hurdling thorny bushes. We made it to the car. "Punch it," Steve said as I jumped in the driver's seat.

Back at our hotel room, I plucked the chiggers from my ankles as Steve inspected the evidence. I wasn't optimistic—we didn't find any evidence that the dogs Baird killed were stolen. Strictly speaking, we couldn't prove he did anything illegal.

"Wait a minute," Steve said, looking at the crumpled papers I had recovered from the pit. "Look at these. Does anything look fishy to you?"

I looked them over. They were official USDA interstate veterinary papers. Whenever a dog was sent to research labs across state lines, a veterinarian had to fill out a form certifying the dog was healthy. In theory, this meant Baird had to hire a veterinarian to examine each of the thousands of dogs he sold every year.

"Look at the signatures," Steve said. "They're all signed by the same vet, in the same ink, dated the same day. There's no way a vet examined every single one of these dogs. I'll bet the vet signs stacks of blank interstate certificates and Baird fills in the information later. That's felony fraud."

"Then we've got him!" I said.

Steve shook his head. "No, we need more proof." He looked at me and smiled. "Feel like going undercover?"

A month later I'd left my home in North Carolina and arrived in Ripley, Mississippi, population: 5,500. Home to myriad fast-food restaurants and trailer parks, Ripley also hosted the First Monday Trade Day, one of the oldest outdoor flea markets in the country. Once a month, merchants descended on Ripley to peddle everything from cars and appliances to, chiefly, animals. People brought thousands of dogs, cats, and birds to Ripley, where they were sold to class B dealers like CC Baird for next to nothing. Baird crossed the border from Arkansas every month with a truck and a wad of ten-dollar bills— that was the going rate for dogs. People who sold to Baird were often destitute and could no longer take care of their pets, but others showed up each month with dozens of well-cared-for, almost certainly stolen dogs. Baird bought them every time, no questions asked.

I knew that Baird was a minister back in Arkansas, so I decided to appeal to his Christian sense of charity. I dirtied myself up and dressed in shabby clothing. When the flea market began, I wandered around telling people I was homeless and looking for work. If I was lucky, Baird would bring me back to Arkansas and set me up with a job. It was demeaning, but if it meant saving dogs, so be it. People were surprisingly kind, offering canned goods and clothing. Finally I spotted his wife, Patsy.

"You'll get no charity here," she said. "Go away."

"I'm just looking for a job, ma'am. I'd love to work for your husband. I'm good with dogs."

"Please go away," she snapped, and then walked off. That was it—my first attempt at undercover work had failed. I slunk away and regrouped later that afternoon with Steve.

"Did Baird see you?" he asked.

"No, just his wife."

"Great. Try again. Move to Arkansas and try getting a job at the kennel itself."

I was tempted to quit. I'd already upended my life to catch this man and had nothing to show for it. LCA was broke and couldn't afford to pay me—I'd been going out of pocket. But something about the dogs at the flea market thoroughly agitated me. They were scared and tired and it would only get worse for them.

"Okay," I said. "Let's do this."

A few weeks later I rented a beat-up trailer that reeked of mildew and stale cigarettes in the sticks of Arkansas—the cheapest place I could find. My first job was to come up with a decent cover story. Williford, Arkansas, was a town near the Ozarks of barely one hundred people. No one showed up there without having a good reason. I found a job flipping burgers at a nearby McDonald's and started spreading my story: I got into some legal trouble in Texas and I just wanted to head somewhere quiet where I could earn a paycheck and keep my head down. In a place suffering from an epidemic of meth addiction and grating poverty, my vague story was all too believable. People nodded their heads, and they never asked questions.

I lay low for a few weeks and even joined the local Church of

Christ, knowing Baird was a minister of his own Church of Christ near his kennel. I told people I wasn't getting enough hours from McDonald's and could use a second gig. I mentioned offhand that I used to work at a kennel. That did the trick. "Oh!" a woman who ran a boot shop told me. "I'll introduce you to Mr. Baird. He owns Martin Creek Kennels."

When I met Baird, he frowned and looked me over. For a split second I was afraid he recognized me back from Mississippi. If he did, my backstory would fall apart. I'd shaved my hair, but I could only do so much. But then Baird yawned and shook my hand.

"What's your background?" he asked.

I recited my carefully rehearsed story, but I was having a minor panic attack. I'd been preparing for weeks. What if I blew it now?

Baird cut me off. "All right. Tell me right now: Are you an undercover investigator? Do you work for PETA?"

I blinked and then said evenly: "Uh, no. What's a *pita*?"

Baird chuckled and slapped me on the shoulder. "Never mind. You seem okay enough. Truth is I rarely hire anyone who hasn't grown up in this town. But I need more hands."

"I'm just trying to stay out of trouble, sir. And I know dogs pretty well." Baird bought my story and told me to show up the next morning. I was in.

I quit my job at McDonald's that afternoon and stopped at the post office, where I found a package from Steve. Using the last of LCA's shoestring budget, he bought me an "undercover" camera: a handheld DV camcorder with a plug-in microphone. It was bulky and low-quality, but it would have to do.

I left my trailer as a cold dawn arose, and I drove to Baird's place. As I approached the kennels a dog began barking, and then a dozen, and then a hundred, as if I were the first person they'd seen in ages. I met the other workers, who showed me the ropes. My job was to be a "hose man," responsible for cleaning the kennels and feeding the animals—essentially the work everyone else avoids. But my real job was to secretly acquire evidence. First I needed to demonstrate that Martin Creek Kennels was regularly abusing animals. Then I had to prove Baird was engaging in felony fraud by falsifying interstate veterinary records; these were the forms I found in the trench. I needed to find stacks of blank forms signed by a corrupt vet—think of them as signed blank checks—proving that Baird never actually had his dogs examined by a veterinarian, as required by federal law.

My first objective didn't take long to complete. The dogs were stuffed into cages five at a time and immediately forgotten. Animals with fleas or ticks were tossed into tanks of permethrin, which burned their eyes and any open wounds. The dogs were underfed and never allowed to run around, which meant they quickly got bored. That is a recipe for disaster for animals who have not been properly socialized. Baird's dogs got into fights, ripped ears off, developed terrible infections that were never cared for. Occasionally workers decided that a dog was too "dangerous" and they were pulled from their cages and shot point-blank with a .22 rifle. About ten dogs died per week, either from lack of food or water, disease, gunshot, or from fights with other dogs. Their bodies were merely plucked from the cages and thrown into trenches like the one I had seen months earlier. If they had heartworms, Baird sold them to research labs.

The few workers Baird employed were overwhelmed by the sheer number of dogs at the kennel. Every week there were more than a hundred new animals arriving, and they were barely inspected before being crammed into cages. They were brought by bunchers, and I could tell instantly from their friendly, socialized demeanor that many of them were very recent family pets. They were almost certainly stolen. Some knew traditional commands; others wanted to approach and lick me and lie in my lap. I wanted so bad to return their love. But as an undercover investigator I was assuming the identity of a careless, negligent redneck who saw dogs as objects, not friends.

On my first day, I was nearly made. Baird's wife, Patsy, walked by as I was entering the kennel from a lunch break. She looked at me and froze. Despite my best attempts at changing my appearance, she recognized me. She hurried off to the house, and I began panicking. *What will Baird do to me?* Then my imagination went wild: *There are guns everywhere. The nearest police station is miles away. What if . . .*

Before I had a chance to run, CC Baird stormed out of the house and confronted me. "Son, I need to ask you something. Have you ever been to Ripley, Mississippi?"

One of the abilities I honed early in my career was to look and sound stupid—perhaps the most important skill an undercover investigator must cultivate. "Um, no," I said slowly, densely. "Where is that?"

"My wife said you approached her looking for work. She said you looked homeless. But you said you're from Texas." He looked at me sternly. "If you're some sort of undercover activist, you better tell me, boy."

"I don't know anything about that, Mr. Baird. I'm just here to work and get paid."

It was her word against mine. Baird stared at me for another second and then smiled. "Hell. You know women. They imagine the craziest things."

He walked off and I finally exhaled. The fact that Baird believed a total stranger over his wife of forty years told me a lot about the man. I was safe for the moment, but I had to be careful. Baird would be watching me.

My cheap undercover camcorder wasn't helping things. It kept cutting out and buzzing and failing at the worst moments. Sometimes abuse I thought I had filmed turned out to be a garbled mess, or upside down, or a six-hour documentary on my underwear. I woke up hours early every day to set up the equipment, which involved duct-taping wires and battery packs to my skin and wearing two pairs of jeans to hold it all. I felt like an Oompa Loompa. Once I was nearly exposed by an errant flash that came from a disposable camera I kept in a pocket, and another time by wires dangling from my pocket. But I was patient. Every day I learned new techniques and I became more comfortable.

I wanted so bad to help the dogs, to gather them in my arms and find them good homes. But I had to keep acquiring evidence. LCA had been in touch with the US Attorneys Office, and while they were skeptical at first, they had agreed to take on the case. But they needed more evidence of abuse—several months' worth—so each day I strapped on my hidden camera and watched dogs being punched and kicked and starved. I watched dogs destroy themselves from the grinding, inhumane boredom associated with prolonged confinement. Others were merely shot so Baird could make a few bucks from their heartworms. They were the lucky ones. Dogs who survived Baird's kennel were sold to research labs, where they were subjected to entirely new kinds of horror. Purebreds, mutts, big dogs, small dogs—they all churned through Baird's kennel and were pawned off to university labs and cosmetic companies and pharmaceutical conglomerates.

I tried not to get attached to the individual dogs. Steve had warned me that any acts of compassion could blow my cover. Baird was on high alert for activists and his wife already suspected me, so I couldn't afford to be seen slipping a starving dog extra kibble. My restraint was tested daily, but a beagle named Rebel very nearly made me abandon the investigation entirely.

Rebel was a year or two old and on the small side—maybe eleven or twelve pounds. I called him Rebel because of his refusal to follow the rules of the kennel. He snapped at the kennel workers when they were rough with him. He growled and barked and tried to escape. When I hosed down his pen, he attacked my hose. It was as if Rebel understood his fate and was determined to change it. The other workers punched and kicked him, but that only seemed to embolden his spirit.

One day I noticed a worker collecting Rebel's feces. When I asked why, he replied: "He has tapeworms."

"Should we get him medication?" I asked.

"No, CC sells them to labs. Just ignore it."

I looked at Rebel, who was pacing defiantly around his pen, as if inspecting the fence for weaknesses. Tapeworms can be cured with a single chewable tablet. If left untreated, however, the condition is painful and leads to malnutrition, which can be fatal in a place like Martin Creek Kennels. But instead of curing Rebel, Baird wanted to make a few bucks by selling his stool.

Rebel's condition worsened over the ensuing days. Every day I'd come in to hose down his pen and notice another rib showing. He still strutted around, ready to fight back, but he was weakening. His barks were hollow and shrill. Soon he stopped barking altogether. I wanted so desperately to help him. Every day I thought, *I can still get him to a vet*. But as Steve told me, "Remember, you're an undercover investigator. Your priority is the case and the case alone. You can save one dog now or a thousand dogs later." If I saved Rebel it would blow my cover and prevent me from acquiring crucial evidence against Baird. And so I made the most difficult decision I've ever had to make: I did nothing. I did nothing as Rebel grew skinnier and weaker. I did nothing as the employees harvested his worm-infested stools. By the end, he didn't even get up when I entered his pen; his piercing eyes gazed at me, still full of life even though his body was not. Finally, on the morning of February 3, I found Rebel dead in his wooden hutch, a shell of his former self. In my notes I referred to Rebel by his USDA tag: no. 35330. But in my heart, he would always be Rebel.

On my off days I met with the US Attorneys Office to go over the case. We finally had enough video evidence of abuse, but the attorney needed the blank veterinary forms to prove Baird was committing interstate fraud when he sold his dogs. The abuse might have netted him a fine, but felony fraud would shut him down for good and possibly put him behind bars. But I had no idea where he kept the forms. He lived with his family on the property. I couldn't simply wander in and search his house.

Four months into the case I finally got my chance when Baird and his wife left town for a few days to visit their grandkids. The next day I arrived early to work and wrapped plastic ziplock bags around my shoes to avoid leaving a muddy trail in the house. I scurried inside through the back door and found Baird's office. I looked through stacks of papers heaped on desks. Then, inside Patsy's desk drawer, I saw a stack of USDA papers. They were blank except for the pre-signed veterinarian signatures. At long last we had our evidence. I took a flurry of photographs and left the property.

I went straight to the US Attorneys Office and entered her office like a conquering hero. In the euphoric haze, my twenty-three-year-old brain expected her to assemble the troops for a raid that very day. They didn't. In fact, they waited six months. Finally, a team of federal investigators raided Martin Creek Kennels and removed 125 dogs who were starved, beaten, and in need of immediate medical attention. But Baird was allowed to keep his USDA license. The fraud investigation was still ongoing, and Baird could continue acquiring dogs and selling them to research labs.

Another year passed. LCA conducted a number of covert interviews with bunchers admitting they routinely stole pets from homes and sold them to Baird, who never asked questions. I struggled to sleep at night knowing that Baird's operation was continuing, that dogs were being stolen, tortured, shot, and peddled off into medical and cosmetic research. Federal investigators had retrieved 125 dogs and sent them to rescue agencies, but what about the thousands more who churned through Baird's illegal operation?

As I've seen over and over, animal cruelty cases take forever to pursue. Federal prosecutors have a full docket of homicide and narcotics cases that take precedence, so I calmly waited as the Baird case wound its way through the justice system. Every few weeks I called to check on the status, and each time I received the same answer: "The investigation is ongoing." But I was hopeful: The US Attorneys Office would not have worked with me unless it believed in this case.

Finally, nearly two years after my investigation, the federal government filed felony fraud criminal charges against CC Baird. The USDA revoked his license, and his operation was effectively shut down. Federal investigators staged a substantial raid and removed more than six hundred dogs from Baird's property and sent them to rescue organizations including DogsOnly, an all-volunteer charity based in Little Rock, Arkansas. Baird and his family were banned for life from operating a kennel, forced to sell seven hundred acres of their property, and they were fined $267,000—at that time the largest fine ever for violations of the USDA's Animal Welfare Act.

But what about the dogs? Many of the pets were stolen from all across the country, and their owners could not be located. Others were strays who'd never had a home. LCA and DogsOnly decided to hold a massive rescue festival at a park in Little Rock. Volunteers took photographs of the dogs and posted them online. When news of Baird's conviction landed, people from all over the country descended on Little Rock to adopt the dogs. Vegan activists flooded in from Vermont and mingled with red-state hunters. Atheists and devout Christians exchanged housebreaking advice. People who would normally loathe one another were united by the common goal of finding homes for abused animals.

Dogs like Justice, Georgia, and Bingo found loving homes. Justice, a black Lab mix, came to her new home petrified of humans and immediately hid under the bed, but with care and patience he became a loving, sweet, and gentle friend. Georgia, a beagle, was so timid she would tremble at the sound of human voices and perennially keep her tail between her legs. But with constant care and affection, she transformed into a beautiful, social animal who craved affection. Bingo, a black shepherd mix, morphed from a fearful, seemingly aggressive dog into a "gentle, wise, loving, loyal, and very silly" friend, according to her rescuer.

On cold mornings, when the frost-glazed grass twinkles as the sun peaks over the horizon, I still think about a spunky little beagle named Rebel. My footage of Rebel's worsening condition and eventual death was key evidence against Baird. I wasn't able to help Rebel, but Rebel was able to help Justice, Georgia, Bingo, and the hundreds of other dogs who were rescued from Baird's property. His death was needless, but it was not in vain.

THE PERFECT PUPPY

Investigating America's Puppy Warehouse

The town of Goodman, Missouri, can be generously described as a speck on a map. Located in the southwest corner of the state, about a hundred miles north of the Ozarks, barely a thousand people call Goodman home. It's perhaps most famous for occasionally popping up on the local news after a tornado tears up a trailer park. Less well-known about this 1.3-square-mile town: It was the nexus of America's puppy mill industry.

About a year after finishing the Baird case, I wanted as much time working in the field as possible. Steve Garrett had left LCA to pursue more work as a private investigator, and I was intrigued by how he worked for himself. Rather than being someone's employee, he had clients. I wanted to do the same thing in the animal rights movement to cut out bureaucracy and focus on fieldwork. But finding clients was difficult—you can't just put "freelance undercover puppy mill investigator" on your LinkedIn profile. Few people understood what I was doing. But eventually a friend told me about a nonprofit dedicated to fighting puppy mills called the Companion Animal Protection Society, or CAPS. I learned CAPS had more experience than any group investigating these mills but had never done employment-based investigations like the Baird case. I saw an opportunity.

Being self-employed, I needed a name for my new "company." Steve told me that he once considered naming his company Point Man Investigations, but the name was never officially used. So I snatched it, with his blessing. I was now the proud owner of an unlicensed, unregistered, unofficial business called Point Man Investigations. The name had no use on IRS forms or checks, but it sounded cool. CAPS agreed to take me on; as it turned out, they had been waiting for someone like me. And they had a target in mind.

After numerous investigations in the early 2000s, CAPS discovered that one company seemed to be buying an enormous number of dogs from breeders all over the country. Puppy mills from Pennsylvania to Oklahoma to Texas were bringing dogs by the truckload to the tiny town of Goodman, home of the Hunte Corporation—the largest class B broker in the country. From Hunte, these puppies were shipped off to pet stores nationwide. Located a few hundred miles from the geographic center of the United States, Hunte was ideally situated to supply tens of thousands of puppies to America's pet stores every year.

Hunte had been on CAPS's radar for an undercover case since 2003, when state inspectors cited the company for illegally dumping more than a thousand pounds of dead puppies in a mass grave, like something out of a Stephen King novel. I could work my entire life and only manage to shut down a handful of the estimated ten thousand puppy mills in the US, but exposing Hunte—the single largest buyer of puppy mill dogs—could do major damage to the industry.

First, I had to get a job there.

Hunte had been unsuccessfully targeted by other activist groups before, so I knew they were on high alert for undercover investigators. I had to be careful about where I'd live: Goodman is not a place

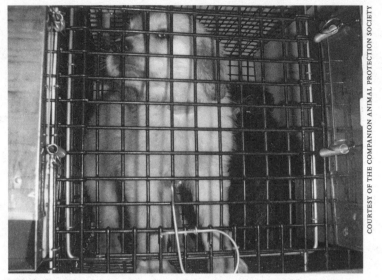

While loading puppies into trucks at Hunte, I would sometimes quickly snap photographs of puppies' cramped conditions. Puppies suffered this confinement while being driven across multiple states to pet stores.

you choose to come to—it's a place you end up. I eventually found a duplex about twenty minutes north in a small town called Neosho. Not too close, not too far. *Duplex* was actually a charitable term: One side was habitable, but the other side was used by the landlord to store moldy furniture and building supplies. I had stayed in far worse, so I signed a month-to-month lease. The landlord had a shed where I could store my dirt bike, and he even let me ride the trails on his sprawling property. I picked up a few basics at the local market—old chairs, a couch, a card table—and presto: a home.

The next day I drove along a dusty, potholed road into Goodman. The main drag had a Baptist church, and across the street was the rival Trinity Pentecostal church. A few blocks away, the Word and Spirit Revival Tabernacle. A liquor store. A restaurant called Redneck Catfish and BBQ, next door to the mini-mart. It looked like your typical rural Midwestern town—that is, until I pulled up to the Hunte Corporation.

A building the size of three dozen houses sat atop a sprawling sea of concrete. A parade of trucks and vans were entering the lot, all waiting their turn to unload cages of yapping puppies. This was like no puppy mill I had ever seen. Most puppy mills are a one- or two-person operation run out of a converted barn with maybe a part-time employee paid off the books. The Hunte facility looked like it was built for one sole purpose: to house and transport as many puppies as possible. Dozens of employees buzzed around, rolling cages in and out of the facility. Small-time breeders from out of town arrived with their most recent litter. For many, their entire livelihood was based on Hunte buying their puppies.

I found my way to the human resources department. A kindly middle-aged woman passed me an application. She eyed me as I filled it out. Hunte paid minimum wage—$5.15 back then—meaning it wasn't the kind of place out-of-towners flocked to for a big opportunity. By far the biggest employer in town, Hunte almost exclusively employed recent high school graduates who had nowhere else to go. I could tell immediately that this woman didn't trust me.

"Thanks for your interest," she said sweetly. "We don't have any openings at the moment, but we'll be in touch."

I called CAPS's founder, Deborah, from the highway. "I'm not sure this is going to work out. They'll never hire me."

"Just keep trying," Deborah said. "Don't worry—you have a way with people."

It was true—I do have an ability to get people to trust me. All good undercover investigators have this skill. The key to selling a convincing lie is not always what you say but what you don't say. If you're a twenty-four-year-old dude looking for a minimum-wage job at a puppy mill in Nowhere, Missouri, you need to have exhausted every last option. A few scrapes with the law, a drug problem, a stint in jail—the key to a good cover story is intimating a troubled past without saying it.

I decided to go for broke. I turned my truck around and headed back to Hunte.

The HR woman frowned at me when I entered her office. "Listen," I said with a calculated hint of desperation in my voice. "I know you don't have any jobs open. I know I don't have a whole lot of experience." I stammered once or twice, flicked my eyes around the room. I noticed the nameplate next to her keyboard: CINDY. I took a deep breath and made eye contact with her. "Hi, Cindy. Listen, I know you're not hiring right now, but I just wanted to make sure to let you know that I am a hard worker. To be honest, I'm having a tough time and I really need this job. I don't show up late. I don't show up drunk. I appreciate you taking my application, ma'am."

Cindy stared at me for a beat, and then she smiled warmly. I knew I was in, right at that moment. In a place like Goodman, where 20 percent of the population was under the poverty line, where methamphetamine addiction was skyrocketing, where everyone seemed to fall through the cracks—Cindy could fill in the rest of my story on her own. She trusted me because she already knew me all too well. Maybe she had a brother, a nephew, or even a son like me. I needed a second chance, and it would be our little secret. I felt a pang of guilt: Cindy was a kind woman who only wanted to help me. I gained her trust by acting vulnerable, by pretending to have problems that are all too common in places like Goodman. I'd come there to help dogs, not deceive good people—but I had no other choice.

Cindy pulled aside a manager. "Why don't you give this young man a tour?" The manager's name was Stephanie, and she gave me a brief history of the operation. In 1991, businessman Andrew Hunte bought Sundowner Kennels and renamed it the Hunte Corporation. By the mid-2000s, Hunte had more than 250 employees and had boosted his revenue thirty-five-fold. Hunte had expanded to an 80,000-square-foot facility, and they were in the process of expanding again to a 135,000-square-foot compound. They needed all the space they could get: At any one moment, there were approximately three thousand puppies kept in stacked cages. Within days most would be gone, shipped to pet stores across the country, and more puppies were brought in.

I had never seen anything like it. There were stacks upon stacks of cages as far as I could see. Row after row, aisle after aisle, like the warehouse from *Raiders of the Lost Ark*. But the memory that sticks with me the most is the barking. Three thousand puppies yelping, yapping, woofing, barking, snapping, and whimpering—all day, every day. The canine symphony echoed against the walls of the warehouse, through the rafters, against the linoleum floor, into my ears. As she gave me the tour, Stephanie had to yell to keep herself heard.

"You get used to it eventually," she hollered cheerfully. *More like you go deaf eventually*, I thought.

I was also struck by how clean the facility was. Most puppy mills I've been to are squalid places: The cages are caked in feces, the runs are cracked and stained, the dog bowls covered in mud. The dogs have never been washed, their fur is matted. But at Hunte, cleaning crews roamed the aisles, sweeping away poop, refilling water bottles, and disinfecting doggy bowls. Overhead, massive fans circulated the air. Despite housing three thousand dogs, the place smelled surprisingly good.

Stephanie brought me to a smaller waiting area, where breeders sat nervously. They had arrived earlier in the day with their puppies, who were being examined by Hunte Corporation veterinarians. If the dogs didn't look like their breed should, Hunte wouldn't buy them—or offer next to nothing—and a breeder might not make his next car or mortgage payment. Some lived nearby, but other breeders had sent puppies from as far as Pennsylvania. For many small-time breeders, this moment makes or breaks their year.

For an undercover investigator, gaining the trust of your fellow employees means finding something in common, whether it's sports, TV shows, or politics. At factory farms I'd investigated, it often meant dropping my r's and brushing up on my history of the Dallas Cowboys. But the Hunte Corporation proved to be a special challenge. Nearly all the workers had grown up together in Goodman, gone to the same high school, drank at the same bars, got into the same sort of trouble. There was a childhood comradery you can't fake. To them, I was an outsider who showed up in town one day desperate to work at a job that carried about the same cachet as flipping burgers at McDonald's. Whenever I turned around I'd catch the eye of some nineteen- or twenty-year-old who was probably thinking, *What the hell did he do to end up here?*

And nearly every employee was dating or married to another employee. This proved most problematic of all. Almost all the men worked on the cleaning crew and all the women worked on the puppy crew—feeding them, transporting them, grooming them, and filling out cage cards. Since my goal was to determine where these animals came from, how well they were treated, and where they ended up, I requested to be put on the puppy crew. The men immediately hated me. Not only was I a stranger from out of town, but apparently I was going to steal their wives and girlfriends.

It was especially difficult given that my previous undercover assignments involved much higher degrees of risk taking. At Martin Creek Kennels, I fed off the adrenaline of sneaking into places I shouldn't be. At Hunte, the greatest danger was pimply, insecure teenagers. Instead of cloak-and-dagger work, I had to navigate drama and learn how to get people to trust me. Initially I found this boring, but the next few weeks turned out to be the most important in my career. Learning to get along with people might not seem like the sexiest skill set when it comes to undercover work, but every investigator must master the art of blending in.

Hunte brought in every dog breed imaginable, and I also spent time learning about each one. After centuries of inbreeding, pure-bred breeds are susceptible to specific issues. For instance, I learned that the eyelids of almost all English bulldogs, French bulldogs, Boston terriers, and pugs need to be sliced shortly after birth so their eyes don't bulge out of their sockets. Their noses must also be cut, or "tacked," so that they can breathe. Great Danes, pit bulls, Dobermans, schnauzers, and many other breeds typically undergo a procedure called ear cropping, which involves surgically altering a dog's pinna (ear flap) into a more "desirable" shape. Some countries have banned the incredibly painful practice, but ear croppings are common in the United States, considered by the American Kennel Club to be "acceptable practices integral to defining and preserving breed character and/or enhancing good health." Small-time breeders often attempt to crop ears themselves, resulting in horrible infections.

I also gained access to paperwork revealing where every dog came from and where they ended up. Every puppy had a cage card that included the breeder's last name, the breed of the puppy, and any veterinary notes, such as if the puppy needed to have her ears cropped or a hernia fixed. By discreetly writing down all this information, I developed a comprehensive list of breeders' names, addresses, and USDA license information. And when my coworkers left for smoke breaks, I'd photograph binders of records that detailed every single pet store Hunte sold to. From tiny mom-and-pop stores to massive chains like Petland, Hunte was the number-one supplier of puppies in the United States. If you walked into a pet store anywhere in America, chances are you were looking at puppies who passed through the Hunte Corporation in Goodman, Missouri.

My first friend was a woman named Laura, a gentle soul whose mere presence was often enough to calm even the most anxious dogs. Despite the systemic issues at Hunte, I was glad that Laura was there to make these animals' lives just a little bit easier. I heard she

In a typical puppy mill whelping pen in Millersburg, Ohio, this Shiba Inu mother's boredom and anxiety were evident from the teeth and claw marks covering her wooden walls and puppy nursing box.

was physically abused by her husband, and I noticed she wore long-sleeved shirts when everyone else had short sleeves. I wanted to help her go to the police, but I worried she would never agree to press charges.

Then there was Stephanie's daughter, Amanda, who was eighteen years old with a new baby girl. She was married to Matt, who worked on the cleaning crew. Combined, the two barely made twelve dollars an hour, and like so many people in this part of the country, they were struggling mightily. I knew early on that Amanda had a tiny crush on me.

Oh, great, I thought. *What if the entire company starts thinking I'm a homewrecker?*

Many of the workers resented Amanda, believing she was in her position only because her mother managed the kennel. On top of that, she was a teenager with a baby. Nobody could understand how hard her life was, so I went out of my way to be kind to her.

After a few weeks on the job, things started getting weird. One day while I was preparing cage cards, Stephanie burst into the warehouse like Paul Revere, hollering, "The USDA is coming! The USDA is coming!" Once a year, the US Department of Agriculture inspects federally licensed breeders and brokers. The visits are supposed to be random, but puppy mills are often tipped off before the inspector arrives so they can clean up their act. This time, however, Hunte apparently missed the memo.

By law, the company was only supposed to have two puppies per cage, but Hunte had as many as five crammed in each one. "Holy shit," Stephanie said. "We need to move these puppies *right now*. I'll stall the USDA guy." She scurried off, and we got to work removing hundreds of puppies from their cages. I watched as employees shoved them into other cages, random hallways, and rooms the inspector had already visited—it didn't even matter if healthy dogs were mixed with sick dogs. When the inspector left one room, Stephanie would distract him and we'd shuffle the dogs back to their original cages like some bizarre game of canine musical chairs.

Everything about the Hunte Corporation seemed fairly legitimate until this point—it was relatively clean and well managed, but something shady was happening.

My next goal was to gain access to the veterinarians, who spent every second of their day examining puppies. They oversaw all the dogs who came in from breeders, and once a week they inspected all outgoing puppies destined for pet stores. Yet only a handful of vets were tasked with examining three thousand puppies a week and signing individual certificates of veterinary inspection, also called CVIs, so they could be sold to the public. Even sketchier, nearly a thousand puppies at any given time were segregated from the others.

The management was tight-lipped about why this was the case, but I suspected these animals had severe health issues. A sick puppy now and then is normal—but a third of the entire population perpetually in quarantine? Definitely not normal.

The company was obsessed with keeping every dog, cage, and bowl squeaky clean, which meant there was a posse of Windex-clutching men in virtually every room of the building. If I could get on the cleaning crew, I could hang around the veterinarians and discover why so many puppies were constantly sick, and if any fraud was occurring. But this meant working next to the men on the cleaning team, who now seemed convinced I was plotting to run away with the entire female population of the Hunte Corporation. I needed an in. But whenever I tried talking to the men, I'd get the narrowed eyes, pursed lips, and reluctant grunts of a stoic Midwesterner too polite to tell you how much he hates your guts.

I finally got a lucky break when I pulled into work one morning at the same time as a worker named Jack, who worked on the cleaning crew. I had heard him talking about his dirt bike. This was my chance.

"Hey, man. I hear you ride a dirt bike," I said.

"Yeah, I guess. Do you?"

"Sure do. I have a YZ250."

Jack looked at me skeptically and glanced around. "Oh yeah?" he said. "You still ride?"

"Hell yeah. We should head out sometime. There a good place near you?"

Jack scratched his head. "Yeah, it's all right. Some nice jumps."

"Listen, I'm no pro, but I love air. Anything with air time is what I'm all about. If you ever want to ride, let me know."

Some of the other guys were looking at us with bemused expressions. They probably figured I'd show up on an old, beat-up motorcycle or a kid's bike. Jack grinned and agreed to meet the next day. He and the other guys walked off laughing.

The next day I showed up at Jack's property expecting a decent motocross track—maybe some basic doubles that were twenty to sixty feet long. The "track" turned out to be a farm field with jumps the size of speed bumps. When I rolled up in my Kevlar pants, padded shirt, body armor, riding boots, and full-faced helmet, Jack stared at me wide-eyed. He had on a tattered jean jacket and an open-faced helmet that looked better suited for after-school rollerblading.

"Holy shit," he said. "I didn't realize I was riding with a motocross pimp!"

I realized all I had to do was be nice to Jack and he wouldn't be intimidated by my bike. Jack wasn't much into racing, but he seemed happy I was attacking his trail like it was a full-on competition. The next day, Jack told the cleaning crew about my riding. Won over by my apparent machismo, they began including me in their conversations, telling me about their lives, their families, their problems. I became particularly friendly with an eighteen-year-old named David. He was a good kid with a rough home life. He was unfailingly patient and sweet when handling the puppies, but he had terrible anger issues with people. One day he didn't show up for work; I later heard he had gotten mad, punched a wall, and broken his hand. I never saw him again.

Even after years of undercover work, I'm still amazed by how people learn to trust one another. It's not necessarily earned with words or actions—trust is won through shared experiences and quiet moments. The everyday people who worked at Hunte weren't sadistic animal abusers; they were kids barely out of high school trying to scratch out a living. At Hunte, they were needed. They were essential. Who doesn't want that?

I finally joined the cleaning crew after getting to know Jack and his friends. Each day, every room that held puppies was thoroughly cleaned. The veterinarian stations especially were deep cleaned to remove any contamination. Every surface, every utensil was cleaned, every speck of dust removed. Tom, the cleaning manager, told me: "Floor to ceiling, wall to wall." He left an impression on me I'll never forget. Some people who do blue-collar work don't like talking about their jobs, sadly believing there is some sort of shame associated with manual labor. Not Tom. If you asked him what he did for a living, he'd look you square in the eye and, enunciating the word clearly, he'd say, "Cleaning." Tom loved explaining it in detail. He was an excellent leader. Everyone on his team respected him and could problem-solve how to deal with unforeseen problems, such as a room overcrowded with puppies or a messy chemical spill. It wasn't lost on me that Tom was the only African American Hunte employee. I've seen a lot of racism from puppy millers in rural areas. I saw none of that toward Tom.

Each worker had a holster of cleaning fluids every color of the rainbow—degreasers, solvents, ammonia, citric acid, bleach. The crew was quiet and efficient, attacking each room with their spray bottles and wiping down every last inch of surface area. In the years since the Hunte case, this quiet work ethic has stuck with me. *Floor to ceiling, wall to wall.* No bullshit, no corner cutting. Just do your job the right way, every day. With all the personal problems these employees had to endure—whether it was a bad marriage, bad parents, no money, drug abuse—they were able to compartmentalize and effectively do their job, no excuses. Tom himself was going through anger management, and he wasn't ashamed to admit it. Even though they were paid barely minimum wage, the men on the cleaning crew took a certain pride in their work that I rarely come across.

My crew was also responsible for loading puppies into trucks bound for pet stores across the country. Before they could leave the facility, the dogs were brought to one of four veterinary stations, where they were checked once more for health problems. In theory, vets were supposed to sign a CVI for each dog, which is required by federal law. As I documented with my undercover camera, there were usually only two vets checking dogs at any one time, typically for a maximum of five seconds. The other stations were manned by members of the cleaning staff or kennel workers—people clearly not certified to be filling out and signing CVIs. As it turned out, they used a rubber stamp with the vet's signature.

This was clearly illegal. But the problems didn't stop there. Whenever puppies showed signs of being sick, the veterinarians tossed them into quarantine. It didn't matter if they had parasites, parvovirus, coccidium, kennel cough, or heartworms. It didn't matter how contagious the dogs were; the vets simply tossed them into quarantine and pumped them full of antibiotics. Some puppies lived, some puppies died.

By the time I understood the full enormity of the situation of the Hunte Corporation, I had been working undercover for six months. I was worn out. We had enough footage to expose the company's fraud, so it was time to make an exit. In most undercover cases, I disappear as quickly as I had shown up—there one day, gone the next. Little good comes from making a graceful exit. But something about the people of Goodman, Missouri, made me pause. The employees of the Hunte Corporation weren't bad people, and for the most part they were gentle with the puppies and enjoyed working with them. I had gained their trust, and they had gained mine. I wasn't out to harm them.

The Hunte Corporation exploited their workers just as they exploited their dogs. Despite revenues in the tens of millions, Hunte paid its staff a pittance. The company's owner, Andrew Hunte, lived in a gated mansion on the edge of town, like Mr. Burns from *The Simpsons*. He required his employees to attend weekly prayer services in which a pastor extolled the virtues of Andrew Hunte—how blessed he was, how generous he was, how *lucky* the people of Goodman, Missouri, were to work for his company. Every week the message was made abundantly clear: It's okay that you and your family are dirt-poor; it's okay that you have nothing while the man running your company has so much. God wanted it so, and He still loves you.

I decided to invent a story so I could leave on good terms. I gave my two-week notice and told everyone that my mother had a serious health problem. I had to head back to North Carolina to take care of her. I hinted that my family members were suffering from drug addiction, and they needed me to run the family construction business. It was a weak story that was full of holes, but no one had any reason to doubt it.

On my last day of work, Amanda presented me with a plastic jar stuffed with small bills, about $200 in total. Even though these people were barely making enough to survive, they genuinely wanted to help me. Later that day I called the CAPS attorney and asked what I should do. "Well, it's not illegal for you to keep that money," he said. "But it would be pretty damn unethical."

The day I left, I stopped over at Amanda's house. I had gotten to know her and her family well over the months. "Listen," I told her. "I can't really get into why . . . but I don't need this money. The truth is, my parents have enough money to take care of each other, but a lot of people here don't have enough money to take care of themselves. I want you to have it. Please take it, and don't tell anyone. Maybe give some to Laura. She's having a hard time."

I felt terrible watching Amanda hold that sad, scratched-up plastic jar full of crumpled one- and five-dollar bills. For many, $200 is a rounding error. But for the people of Goodman it was enough to pay rent for one more month, a car payment, or a temporary reprieve from the debt collectors who call deep into the night. It's a babysitter so Mom can enjoy a night out at the nicest restaurant in town.

Amanda couldn't argue with me, of course. She was a broke, eighteen-year-old mother. She simply stared as I turned around and walked back to my truck. She was still standing there when I turned the corner. I couldn't bring myself to wave.

CAPS released my footage online following the Hunte Corporation investigation. Sensing momentum, other activist groups began their own investigations of the company. A few years later, the Humane Society of the United States filed a class-action lawsuit against the Hunte Corporation and Petland for conspiring to sell unhealthy puppies to unsuspecting consumers in twenty states.

As Hunte continued to attract bad press, pet stores slowly but surely began sourcing from other brokers. In 2005, just after I was undercover at Hunte, the company sold more than 88,000 puppies. Three years later, that figure had dropped to about 72,000. Thanks to the hard work by activists, many of the largest pet markets, such as California and New York, have imposed strict standards that prevent stores from sourcing puppies from massive class B brokers like Hunte. In recent years, Hunte has attempted a rebranding. Today, the company is known as Choice Puppies, although the company's volume and revenues have dwindled substantially. In 2015, it sold just 34,000 puppies.

Hunte and other class B brokers are losing the war of attrition against anti-cruelty legislation and the rescue dog movement. I'm proud of the role I've played in this fight. The Hunte Corporation was a front for the puppy mill industry, the middleman that connected puppy mills in Middle of Nowhere, Minnesota, with massive store-fronts in New York. We also discovered that a significant number of puppies were sick upon arrival. Some may have become ill while at Hunte, but it was clear many of these puppies were arriving there sick. Hunte merely got them healthy enough to peddle off to a pet store, which in turn would peddle them off to consumers who didn't know any better. Hunte promised they sourced puppies from only the best breeders, but based on the condition of these animals, that clearly wasn't the case. My next step was to visit the breeders I had uncovered who supplied Hunte. Hundreds of names were on my list. For the next several years I would devote myself to visiting many of these kennels—the seedy underbelly of the puppy mill industry.

In nearly all my cases there is a dog who sticks out, if only briefly. Sometimes I'm able to rescue him or her, most times I'm not. Like Rebel and Spot and the other dogs in this book, I remember my experiences through them. But Hunte was unique. Three thousand dogs came and went every week. Each and every one of them were sold to pet stores around the country. Blink and they're gone. A fresh new batch of golden retrievers and huskies and Chihuahuas are there tomorrow, and then three thousand more the next week. Hunte's motto at the time was "the perfect puppy." The company's website claimed that "All Hunte puppies come from breeders that meet or exceed federal requirements." They were of perfect health with a perfect pedigree from perfect breeders. But just like the shiny exterior of the Hunte Corporation itself, the truth about Hunte's puppies is far more sinister. As I would discover investigating the breeders who supplied Hunte, the reality of where these puppies came from was anything but perfect.

SUGAR

The Truth About Pet Store Puppies

I pulled off US 77 about thirty miles east of Wichita, Kansas. A few stunted trees dotted the parched, endlessly flat landscape. A truck rumbled by, a cloud of dust lingering in its wake. I opened my wrinkled Hagstrom map to get my bearings—this was 2004, before iPhones and turn-by-turn GPS directions. There was no official exit on the highway, just a gravel road leading to a large fenced property. A name in faded black letters painted on the side of a trailer read PS PUPS.

While spending months combing through the pet store paperwork I had photographed at the Hunte Corporation, I noticed a number of breeders kept popping up again and again. Hunte had claimed to source their dogs from only the most reputable kennels. Neal Spies, the owner of PS Pups, was one of Hunte's star breeders, selling the company hundreds of puppies every year. This could prove to be a major indicator of where Hunte's "perfect puppies" came from—and, by extension, the source of most pet store puppies.

The driveway was blocked by a cattle gate draped with a rusty chain. I removed the chain, opened the gate, and drove onto the property. The yard was littered with old appliances and heaps of

Sugar went from a filthy wire cage of the Spies puppy mill of Augusta, Kansas, to a loving home halfway across the country. Once rescued, she loved to curl up in people's arms or laps and knew nothing but affection.

trash. I saw at least fifty massive outdoor enclosures covered with shredded blue tarp and surrounded by galvanized wire fences.

I parked next to a small house with a sagging roof. The porch creaked under my weight as I approached the front door. Behind the house a single dog barked, and then dozens were yapping and woofing and yelping. Before I could knock, the door swung open. A tall, middle-aged man with thinning gray hair stared at me. His skin was pale and his milky eyes seemed to gaze past me, as if he wasn't entirely aware of my presence. His remaining teeth were stained a deep yellow. From my years working undercover in rural areas, I instantly recognized the face of what I believed to be a methamphetamine addict. I had to be careful.

"Mr. Neal Spies?" I asked evenly.

"Are you with the government?" Spies demanded.

"No, sir." I'd had my cover story planned for days: "My name is Dave, and I'm with a magazine called *Commercial Canine*. I'd love to interview you about your breeding operation." *Commercial Canine* was entirely made-up—a thin cover, but it had worked in the past. "We're a publication for commercial breeders, and we want to profile a successful businessman like yourself."

"See that tree out there?" Spies said, gesturing to a twisted oak about five football fields out. "I was a sniper in 'Nam. I could hit a man standing next to that tree, and I could hit an inspector through the eyes coming past my gate."

"Wow," I said, eyeing the hunting rifle propped up near the corner of the porch. "That's cool."

He continued to size me up as I reflexively yawned—an old undercover trick I learned to pretend I'm not nervous. "So, Mr. Spies. Do you have a few minutes? I'd love to see your kennel and talk about your dogs."

"Yeah, I guess you can see them. But that's not my main business these days. Well, it is, but maybe your magazine can mention my other venture, which I'm tryin' to get started."

I decided to humor him. "Oh yeah?"

"Exorcisms," he replied.

So this is the Hunte Corporation's star breeder, I thought. "Sure . . . we can find some column space for that, I think."

"Tell you what, I'll do one for you right now, free," Spies continued. Suddenly he grabbed my head and drew me close. He smelled of sweat and cat urine, which is also the smell of meth being cooked. He exhaled into my face and released me.

"There you go. You are now blessed. The demon inside you is gone."

Well, at least this trip wouldn't have been a total waste of time, I thought. "Thank you, Neal." My insides were still retching from the smell of his breath.

"You'll write about that in the article, yeah? Mention that I have two fourteen-foot angels standing next to me at all times. Also mention that I'm a prophet. Okay," he added, "now let's do your car."

He strutted to the hood and knelt down, bowing his head, closing his eyes, and murmuring to himself. Then he looked at me brightly and said, "Yes, yes, there you go. I just blessed your vehicle. Now you have angel gas, and you'll have better mileage."

"Even better. I do a lot of driving."

With the demon exorcism and gasoline benediction out of the way, Spies was ready to show me his kennel. He told me that he had 150 breeder dogs including German shepherds, Lhasa apsos, Maltese, shih tzu, miniature pinschers, and beagles. The outdoor pens had dirt floors and were enclosed by wire fences. The dogs jumped and whimpered as I walked by. I silently counted the USDA violations: dogs forced to navigate around weeks-old feces and filthy mud puddles; mud-encrusted water bowls; dogs with matted fur, suggesting they were never washed or groomed; fences with jagged metal wires; cages with no water; sick dogs who had clearly not received veterinary attention; and flies everywhere. A cage holding German shepherds had an inch-thick layer of sawdust and feces caked to the flooring. A tiny hut in the beagle cage couldn't provide shelter for all the animals in case of inclement weather. A miniature poodle leapt as we walked past. Spies responded by throwing a rock at her. She yelped and retreated under a tarp. Spies continued to tell me about his exorcism business and his plans to overthrow the federal government.

The dogs living in these squalid conditions would never be seen by dog owners. They were mothers who were alive solely to give birth. They were impregnated again and again until they were worn out, and then they were killed. Most mothers had given birth to dozens of puppies, each of whom had been shipped off to the Hunte Corporation and other class B puppy peddlers. I had wondered why so many puppies at the Hunte Corporation were sick. Now I had my answer.

Spies walked me to the middle of the kennel yard to another pen. It was tiny—about two feet by four feet. Inside were three Maltese females deftly darting around piles of feces and sawdust. Maltese are beautiful creatures with fluffy white fur and teddy-bear faces. These were tiny, too—barely eight inches long and less than five pounds.

I rescued Teddy from the Van Wyk puppy mill of New Sharon, Iowa, one of the most abhorrent dog kennels I've ever seen. Teddy's only home was once a dark, wire cage, but the Animal Rescue League of Iowa helped him find a loving family.

COURTESY OF THE COMPANION
ANIMAL PROTECTION SOCIETY

"Here, you can write about this in your article," Spies said. "Goddamn Maltese who don't breed." He scooped up one of the squirming dogs. She trembled in his firm grip. "Like this one. Won't breed no more. Totally useless."

I looked at the teensy dog. She was about four years old with enormous dark eyes that reminded me of Japanese anime characters. Maltese are normally fluffy, but her stark-white coat was covered in layers of mud. Her toenails were long and scraggily and hadn't been cut in months.

"No use to me anymore, so I keep her in this cage. I'll put her down soon, I think," Spies said casually.

I knew it would be years before the USDA took action on

unscrupulous breeders like Neal Spies, but I was suddenly deter-mined to do a small kindness for one of these animals.

"No need to put her down," I said, taking the Maltese from Spies. "My mom needs a dog." I felt her tremble, and her paws clung to me as she buried her head in my shoulder.

Spies looked at me curiously but agreed to give me the Maltese. I didn't have the proper supplies in my car, so I arranged to return the following day. As I returned the little dog to her cage, she clawed fe-rociously at my arms. *Don't leave me here*, she was telling me. I scratched her ears and tried to reassure her. "Just one more day," I whispered. "Hang tight."

The next day I returned with a doggy crate, a leash, a harness, kibble, toys, treats, and several large towels. I was worried that Spies had forgotten our arrangement, but to my relief, the little Maltese was still in her pen. Spies and I shook hands, and I placed the little dog in the passenger seat of my car.

"Thanks for everything, Neal," I said. "You can count on a feature article in our magazine."

"Give me a call if that demon comes back," he hollered as I drove off.

A minute later I was speeding down US 77. I looked over at the little dog I had rescued. She was shivering and underfed. I arrived in the nearest town and found a hotel, where I give her a hot bath. Her fur was gnarled and twisted into doggy dreadlocks. I did my best to wash away the dirt, and soon she smelled like a normal dog, her fur glistening white. She looked like a sweet white candy ball. I named her Sugar.

A local dog groomer couldn't do anything about the doggy dreads, so he shaved Sugar's fur. Now she resembled a white Chihuahua rat. I assured Sugar that she'd look beautiful in a few weeks' time. She waited patiently as the groomer finished his work, and then she fell asleep in my arms, her head buried in my elbow.

Like with so many other dogs I've rescued, the primary problem wasn't saving Sugar—it was finding her a home. I was constantly on the road, so I couldn't give Sugar the full-time care she deserved. Fortunately, my parents knew a family looking for a Maltese. I brought Sugar to the vet for her shots, then hopped on a plane to North Carolina. The airline allowed her to travel carry-on in a tiny crate—people mistook her for a cat—but she was not happy being locked up again. She trembled and began to whine, so I stuck my fingers through the cage and pet her for the duration of the trip.

My parents' friend Sandra and her husband, Neil, came to meet Sugar the next day. I was worried they might be turned off because of Sugar's rodent-like appearance, but they immediately fell in love with her. Sugar plopped into Sandra's lap and soaked up the attention.

Like so many rescues I've worked with, Sugar did not understand affection, nor did she understand being fed treats, walking on a leash, playful roughhousing, or fetch. When I threw popcorn, Sugar would just watch the kernel hit her nose. These instincts come, but they take a lot of love and care.

Now Sandra and Neil were helping her make up for lost time. It was a perfect match. Sugar never wanted to be left alone; Sandra always wanted to hold her. Every day Sandra would send me a new photo of Sugar basking in attention and kindness. And with each photo, Sugar's coat was a little thicker and a little whiter. Sandra brought her everywhere—to work, to restaurants, to movies. After a lifetime of being kicked and abused, all Sugar wanted was to be held. For years Sandra would knit Sugar tiny outfits, and when Sugar's health started failing, Sandra bought her diapers. Sugar died in her sleep at age fifteen, ten years after I rescued her. She would not have made it another ten hours with Neal Spies.

———

I wish every puppy mill dog found a loving home like Sugar. Sadly, the vast majority do not. There are an estimated 10,000 puppy mills in the US and 167,000 dogs used for breeding, of whom Sugar was just one. These dogs produce approximately 2 million puppies every year, many living in squalid places just like PS Pups—kennels that make the Hunte Corporation look like a Four Seasons hotel.

People often ask me how this is possible. "Aren't there *laws* against this sort of thing?" they wonder. Of the millions of federal laws on the books, just one protects dogs. The Animal Welfare Act (AWA) was passed in 1966 in response to growing concerns over how dogs and cats were used in exhibition and for research institutions. (In 2002, the law was amended to exclude mice, rats, and birds, meaning 95 percent of research animals are not bound by the statute.)

The AWA mandates basic minimum standards of care, such as cage size, temperature, exercise, breeding frequency, basic hygiene, and socialization. At PS Pups, just like the hundreds of other puppy mills I've visited over the years, there were scores of violations— enough to trigger a massive fine at the very least, if not the termination of Neal Spies's license. Yet Spies had no violations on his record, meaning the USDA, which is in charge of enforcing the Animal Welfare Act, didn't bother to draft a complaint.

The USDA historically has an extremely cozy relationship with the very players they are supposed to be regulating. The "Keep 'Em in Business Act," as activists like to jokingly call the AWA, is purposefully vague and barely enforced by the USDA to keep breeders and research labs happy. By design, the regulations are riddled with loopholes. Under the law, for example, a medium-sized dog could spend her entire life inside a fifteen-square-foot cage without ever leaving— and it would be perfectly legal. Even dogs crammed four or five to a cage don't have to be let out. When it comes to housing, breeders like

Neal Spies are allowed to stack cages of dogs with no solid flooring. The cage wire is supposed to be wide enough to not harm dogs' paws, but USDA inspectors rarely bother to look closely.

The problem stems from the USDA's inherent conflict of interest. After all, the USDA official mission statement is "Helping rural America to thrive [and] to promote agriculture production that better nourishes Americans." As for the Animal and Plant Health Inspection Service (APHIS), the department within the USDA responsible for overseeing dog breeders, its official mission is "To protect the health and value of American agriculture and natural resources." Nowhere is the health and value of the animals themselves mentioned.

APHIS employs barely one hundred inspectors charged with overseeing the nation's three thousand USDA-licensed puppy mills. (The other roughly seven thousand puppy mills are smaller-scale and do not require a federal license to operate.) Inspectors are supposed to conduct surprise inspections at kennels, but these inspectors are overworked and underpaid. They are also responsible for visiting the eight thousand other USDA-licensed facilities that use animals, including circuses and research labs. As a result, the number of actual puppy mill violations reported to the USDA is shockingly low. In 2016, the USDA issued a *total* of 192 written warnings to dog breeders, exhibitors, and research labs, and filed official complaints against just twenty-three. Through the first three-quarters of 2018, the agency filed thirty-nine warnings and just one complaint, which was promptly settled for $2,000. In the meantime, the USDA has removed its once publicly available enforcement records from its website; they are now only available in redacted form from a Freedom of Information Act request, which can take months to process. Most recently, the USDA has been piloting the use of announced inspections, meaning breeders can prepare months in advance for their scheduled visit.

All of this means that breeders like Neal Spies can continue abusing their animals with impunity. It is extremely rare for the USDA to terminate a breeder's license. In 2016 the agency terminated just nine. Since then, that figure is closer to zero. Some states, such as Pennsylvania, California, and New York, have passed their own laws to rein in the worst offenders, but other states, such as Arkansas, don't even require their breeders to be licensed.

Puppy mills proliferate thanks to a culture of lax enforcement at all levels of government. And, as I would soon learn, puppy mills are even protected by the local police.

THE WHITE POMERANIAN

When Law Enforcement Fails to Protect Dogs

n the early hours of November 9, 2016, after the major networks had called the presidential race for Donald Trump, a bleary-eyed, shell-shocked Stephen Colbert was hosting an election-night special, attempting to contextualize the moment. At a loss for words, the comedian finally signed off with a hastily drawn list of things Americans could still agree on that morning: Universal hatred toward people who reply-all to mass emails and universal love for the game show *Jeopardy!* host Alex Trebek notwithstanding, the *Late Show* host could think of few obvious points of consensus.

Actually, I know one thing where practically all Americans can agree: Animal cruelty is bad. The public overwhelmingly supports laws that protect animals from harm. A 2015 Gallup poll found that 32 percent of Americans believe animals should be afforded the same rights as humans, with another 62 percent believing they should have significant protection. Only 3 percent believed animals deserved no protection at all. Many parts of the country, including Tampa, Florida, have even begun online registries that publish the names, photographs, and addresses of convicted animal abusers in much the same way they do for sex offenders.

COURTESY OF THE COMPANION ANIMAL PROTECTION SOCIETY

I was appalled not only by the conditions these dogs lived in at Reuben Wee's puppy mills but by how the conditions were evident even from the highway.

Despite overwhelming public support for basic animal protections, getting laws passed is very difficult. Getting law enforcement to follow through with animal cruelty charges can be even more difficult. I found this out the hard way in rural Balaton, Minnesota.

In the early 2000s a breeder named Reuben Wee was near the top of CAPS's target list. Although he had once been USDA licensed, Wee let his license lapse in 2001. Thereafter, he could legally sell only to the general public, but CAPS discovered that Wee was getting around these restrictions by selling to a broker who then sold to pet stores—a maneuver that breeders often use to avoid USDA inspections. The practice is illegal but few people are ever prosecuted.

In 2001 and 2002, CAPS undercover investigators released footage of the deplorable conditions at Wee's facility and reported their findings to the USDA, which took no action. In 2005, we decided it was time to try again, this time with local law enforcement.

Balaton is a tiny place nestled beside a lake in southwestern

Minnesota. From the sky, the few roads comprising the town look like graph paper—all straight and intersecting at perfect ninety-degree angles. Shoulder-high corn occupies nearly every square foot of land. Most interstate exits are for people's homes, and you can drive a distressingly long distance between gas stations.

Wee's property was located directly off Highway 91. On an unseasonably cold morning in June, I turned off the highway and drove my car down his dusty driveway.

I began spotting violations before I'd even parked. The concrete dog pens were covered in mud, feces, and wispy strands of cornstalks from nearby fields. Skinny miniature pinschers and Pomeranians with wet, matted fur eyed me, tails between their legs, paws scratching along the concrete pens as they paced back and forth. Dog runs like these extended toward the back of the property, near a small white house. A lone van was parked out front.

I pulled up to the house, serenaded by three dozen barking dogs. These were the adult dogs who Wee used for breeding purposes. I knocked on the door. No response. I decided to roll the dice and explore the property, first approaching the Pomeranian and miniature pinscher pens. These were about six feet wide and enclosed with a chain-link fence. The dogs were soaking wet, shivering, and stepping gingerly around piles of weeks-old feces. Their food bowls were caked in mud and filled with waterlogged kibble. The water bowls were stained muddy brown. The Pomeranians were like skittering fluff-balls, the perfect size for breeding teacup puppies that are so often in vogue. They were brown, golden, black, white, and parti-color, meaning white with large black and brown spots. Their fur was so matted they appeared to have long, flat dreadlocks. The miniature pinschers were black and brown with their trademark pointy ears. The dogs were all scratching at sores on their manure-spattered bodies.

A lone white Pomeranian sat on the filthy concrete between a plastic doghouse and wire wall of the run, shivering, refusing to look at me. Other dogs ran up to the wire walls to get as close as possible, while others ran frantic circles around their doghouses. But the white Pomeranian just sat in place, shaking. My mere presence terrified her.

I took photographs of the kennel as if it were a crime scene—which it was. Wee may not have been USDA licensed anymore and was therefore not subject to the Animal Welfare Act, but Minnesota had specific laws about housing, feeding, and providing basic veterinary care for animals. Local authorities would certainly have the right to bring serious charges against him.

Next I walked over to the pens containing the bullmastiffs and boxers. The dogs were standing on a mixture of mud, manure, and water that had solidified into a hard sludge. Cheap plastic doghouses sat toppled in the corners of the pens, but they were too small for any of the dogs to fit inside. The pens were enclosed by wire walls zip-tied together. Bullmastiffs and boxers are large working dogs with scrunched faces and strong muscles. Both breeds are powerful and, like all dogs who receive proper socialization, grow up to become sensitive, sweet family dogs. Working dog breeds require regular exercise, but the ones living at Wee's kennel had likely never left their pens. One bullmastiff eyed me from behind the doghouse. He was about a hundred pounds with a beautiful brown, black, and tan striped coat. His eyes were large and sad, and he padded up to me when I held out my hand. He licked his lips nervously. One of his ankles was swollen to about twice the normal size, clearly an old injury that had never been tended to.

Closer to Wee's house was an old barn. As I approached the sagging plywood doors I could hear panting and shuffling paws. I stepped inside. The air was hot and thick; dust particles danced in the window light. I swung the doors open wider, allowing in enough light to see dilapidated pens along the edges of the barn. This is where Wee kept his puppies. There were a dozen bullmastiff and miniature pinscher puppies scampering along the manure-stained floors. In the far corner, the boxer puppies eyed me warily. Beer cans and cigarette butts lay among a bed of wood shavings. There was dog poop everywhere. At first the puppies edged away from the light, their eyes clearly not acclimated to anything but darkness. Then one yipped, and all at once tiny puppy barks were echoing off the walls. *Time to go*, I thought, taking as many photographs as possible.

As I was leaving, two trash piles at the southeast edge of the property caught my eye. Wee clearly abused his dogs and didn't bother cleaning his kennel, but the property was otherwise well manicured. After conducting scores of undercover cases, I knew what was coming before I saw it. Behind the trash was a long wooden board inside a patch of overgrown grass with a cloud of buzzing flies overhead. With my camera running, I lifted the board to find the remains of two Pomeranians.

I had seen enough. I hustled back to my truck and back to my hotel, where I spent the rest of the day compiling the footage. At five p.m. I dropped the evidence off at the Murray County Sheriff's Office. I made it clear to Sheriff Steve Telkamp that CAPS would be providing the footage to the local press as well as partnering with a local shelter that agreed to take Wee's dogs in the event the sheriff's office raided the property. Telkamp was young with buzzed blond hair and a clean, crisp uniform. He listened politely and then, to my surprise, agreed to visit Wee's property as soon as he could.

True to his word, Telkamp visited the property later that evening. Afterward he called to explain that while he would not be seizing animals immediately, he felt the sheriff's office could bring charges against Wee. I was more concerned with saving dogs than nabbing Wee, but it was a start. "Great!" I told him.

The next day I visited Wee in person, along with staff from the local shelter, Animal Ark, which had offered to take in the dogs. In situations where I know law enforcement is going to press charges, I usually try to help out the offenders. If Wee were to voluntarily give up his animals, I reasoned, I could probably convince Telkamp to drop the case and everyone would go home happy.

When we arrived at the property Wee was standing by his front door. He was about sixty years old, balding, with a modest paunch. Like so many puppy mill operators I've met, at first glance he struck me as quite pleasant, greeting us warmly with aw-shucks mannerisms. I tried to rationalize why he treated his dogs so poorly. He seemed like a perfectly kind man—was he sick, overwhelmed, or just too frail to care for them?

We explained what was going to happen and offered to take his dogs. "We'll make it as easy as possible for you," I said. "They'll get good homes. I think we can agree they are not currently in great shape."

Wee remained calm throughout the conversation, and I felt good about where things were going. But after we relayed our offer, he frowned and said: "Nope, thank you." When I pressed him further, Wee explained that the dogs belonged to his son and daughter. He claimed that only four of them were being used to breed puppies; the dozens of other adults were merely pets.

It's a common trick. In most states, if someone has under five dogs used for breeding, he or she does not have to register as a commercial breeder and therefore is not subject to inspections or regulations under the Animal Welfare Act. Even though there were dozens of dogs on his property, Wee was claiming they were only his children's pets. He might get dinged for an animal cruelty charge—which at the time in Minnesota basically amounted to a fine—but he could go along breeding and selling dogs illegally and no one would care. He had thought this through.

The next day, after driving to the sheriff's office, I explained to Telkamp what I suspected about Wee, expecting him to agree that Wee must be forced to surrender his dogs. Instead, he told me to hold tight.

"We're working on charges," he said. "It might take some time. Then we'll see what we can do about the dogs."

I asked Telkamp what we could do about the dogs now. He looked at me, exasperated. "Look, you got what you want," he said. "We filed the charges. He's gotta stop breeding dogs. As far as I'm concerned, case closed."

"I'm worried that he's just going to shoot his dogs," I pleaded. "There must be something we can—"

"No." He stood up and stared at me calmly but intensely. "*No*. Do not return to the property." He let the sentence hang while he locked eyes with me. I knew what Telkamp was doing. He realized I was talking to the press, and so he didn't want to speak his mind to me. At the same time, he didn't want me gathering more evidence, either. It was a polite way of saying, *"Get the hell out of my county."*

I agreed to let the case run its course—it's always in my best interest to stay on good terms with law enforcement. But I had a bad feeling. Every day that passed with inaction, that white Pomeranian was not getting the medical treatment she needed, the bullmastiff was being forced to eat kibble contaminated with mud and excrement, and another dog was being buried in a ditch. Weeks passed, but nothing happened. Finally, after repeated calls to Telkamp that went unanswered, he gave me an answer: Wee had been charged with a single count of animal cruelty.

However, the sheriff's office would do nothing to verify what action Wee took with his remaining dogs. Was it so much to ask to find a proper home for these animals? What if Wee merely stopped feeding them, or let them loose on the highway? A man who didn't care enough about his animals to properly feed them clearly wouldn't spend time finding them a forever home. I also wondered what Wee would do with the little Pomeranian, whom I'd last seen with her head buried between a wire wall and doghouse. So defenseless and frightened, she would be terrified of being used as a breeder in another puppy mill, and I doubted she would be easily adopted by anyone Wee tried to give his dogs to.

I had to go back. Knowing that Wee would be on the lookout for my car, I had a friend drop me off in front of the property at twilight. I saw from the driveway that the Pomeranian and miniature pinscher pens were empty. So were the boxer and bullmastiff pens. I heard no barking. Even the highway was quiet. The only sound was the soft crunch of mud and grit under my boots. There were no lights on in the house. I walked to the barn and peeked inside—nothing. Weeks earlier there were scores of puppies and their mothers. Now every single one was gone. I approached the trash heap in the back, praying not to see a mass grave. Nothing. Just as I turned back toward the barn, I heard a twig snap. Reuben Wee was staring at me, an enormous bullmastiff by his side.

Wee picked up a shovel that was leaning against the house and paced toward me. Even in the dim twilight I could see his twisted expression. Gone was the kindly, aw-shucks grandpa I had met earlier in the summer. This version of Wee was pure menace.

"What do you think you're doing?" he spat.

"Leaving," I said automatically.

"You're not leaving."

Dogs have an uncanny ability to read the mood of their human companions. This particular bullmastiff snarled and charged just as Wee raised his shovel above his head. I turned toward the woods at the edge of the property and sprinted. I thought that it was over—Wee would lower his shovel and call off his dog, satisfied with my swift departure. Instead, the sixty-one-year-old summoned decades-old muscle memory from an apparent competitive javelin-throwing career and hurled the shovel after me. It careened ten feet through the air like a bolt from a crossbow, sailing inches from my face and embedding itself deep in the ground.

The adrenaline response does curious things to people. After the shovel whizzed by my head, my first thought was to turn around and retrieve the ball cap that I had inadvertently knocked off my head while attempting to flee. *That's my lucky cap*, I thought, before remembering the bullmastiff bearing down on me. Bullmastiffs are famously protective of their masters, no matter if they are small children or puppy mill owners with homicidal tendencies. I left the cap and sprinted through the woods, tripping over logs and hurtling through bushes until my lungs burned.

Eventually I collapsed in a patch of grass several properties down. I had never run so hard in my life. As I was catching my breath, I heard sirens approaching Wee's property. I hadn't called the police, which means Wee had. My only choice was to call the sheriff's office and explain my side of the story. The dispatcher on the other side patiently listened to me and then said, "The sheriff is on his way to pick you up. Sit tight."

This can either go really well or really bad, I thought.

When Telkamp arrived, he produced a pair of handcuffs. I was about to tell him that Wee was back at his house when I realized the handcuffs were for me. Telkamp cuffed and escorted me to the back seat of his cruiser. Once we started moving, he unloaded on me.

"What did I tell you?" he said.

"Sir—"

"What did I tell you?"

I tried to explain what had happened—that I only wanted to see what happened to Wee's dogs, that he had tried to detain and physically harm me. But Telkamp was hearing none of it.

"You activists . . . ," he said, his voice dripping with derision. "It's never enough, is it? You come here and stir up trouble, and then you want to stir up more trouble. Where are the cameras now? Huh? Where's the press you wanted?" He continued to rant about animal rights activists for another fifteen minutes until we reached the station. After processing me, a deputy had me write my statement. I spent two hours painstakingly re-creating the day's events. While Telkamp had told me to stay off the property, Wee had not. Nor did he have NO TRESPASSING signs up on his property. It might not have been the strongest defense, but the truth was a man had attacked me with a shovel after I helped shut down his puppy mill horror show. He wasn't the victim here.

"Okay, you can go," the deputy told me when I finished my statement.

"That's it?" I asked.

He nodded. There were no charges filed—or so I was told. I left the building and left town, hoping never to return to Balaton, Minnesota, ever again.

As for Reuben Wee, he eventually pleaded guilty to one count of animal cruelty. The sentence: a $370 fine. He was also forbidden from keeping more than one dog at his home. In theory, this meant Wee could no longer pretend to be breeding puppies for him and his family. But the odds that he would continue breeding were high. I thought about the female bullmastiffs sidestepping around the filth and the tiny Pomeranians spending their days gnawing on food bowls. They deserved a better fate than to waste away on a farm in Balaton, Minnesota.

About a month later, the Wee case firmly out of my mind, I received a call from a prosecutor at the Murray County district attorney's office. He informed me that I had been convicted of trespassing. I had never been sent a court notice or otherwise informed that I had been formally charged with a crime. I needed to return to Murray County for my sentencing date.

"You didn't show up for your court date," he said. "Therefore you've been convicted. I'm sorry, that's how it works."

Wearily, I told my story once again. I explained why I was in Balaton in the first place, how I had helped the sheriff's office shut down Wee's operation, and how I simply wanted to find the dogs a good home. Like most assistant district attorneys, he had a lot on his plate, so he was happy to play. I agreed to pay a $600 fine and promised to stay out of trouble for a year. I told him that I had no intention of returning to Balaton, Minnesota, for the remainder of my life. Sure enough, the charge was eventually expunged from my record.

I was lucky. The kind of corruption I encountered in Murray County, Minnesota, may seem like an anomaly, but it's all too common in states specializing in animal agriculture. Minnesota ranks second in the nation in hog farming and first in turkey production. Many puppy mills I've visited in the state used to be factory farms. Hog pens are excellent whelping pens for dogs. Farrowing barns, usually set over manure pits, are ideal for storing lots of dogs in cages. At various times the Minnesota legislature has tried to pass so-called ag-gag laws, which would make it a crime to record unauthorized footage inside farms (and, in several states, puppy mills). These laws, which are designed to silence whistle-blowers and penalize activists, have already been passed in Alabama, Arkansas, Iowa, Kansas, Missouri, and North Carolina, while judges have struck down ag-gag laws in Idaho and Utah. These states tend to have the highest concentrations of puppy mills in the country.

Life on farms is hard and stressful. Workers are often sleep deprived and can easily become dehydrated and hungry with little time to take a break. This makes it very easy for workers to become desensitized to animal abuse. Many workers see sick or injured animals who can't walk as simply a problem to kick into place instead of a living being in need of help. None of these reasons are excuses for animal cruelty, but they do help explain why it's so common, and why rural law enforcement so seldom takes action against "minor" cruelty violations.

I can also sympathize with law enforcement officials who don't like the idea of civilian investigators meddling in their jurisdiction. I have no license for what I do. I've invented training programs for numerous animal rights organizations, but I have no formal training. I've seen self-taught activists try to work cases in an unprofessional manner, and as angry as I was at them, I can only imagine how a police officer would feel dealing with them. Nearly half of the activists I've trained eventually quit or were kicked out of training, and that's out of the 1 percent whose applications were accepted. There are no official benchmarks for civilian animal rights investigators. That is our curse and our blessing. If we're unprofessional, we cause problems for law enforcement and the animal rights movement. But if we are professional, bound by few rules and with no limits to jurisdiction, we can uncover criminal animal cruelty wherever we are needed.

In rural areas, county sheriffs play a large role in law enforcement. It's also an elected position, which inevitably means that sheriffs are less likely to enforce laws that could affect them politically. Sheriff Telkamp behaved inappropriately toward me, but he did take action to stop Reuben Wee from continuing to breed dogs. In many other places in the country, nothing would have happened at all.

I never found out what happened to the little white Pomeranian from Wee's property, or any of the other dogs imprisoned in his puppy mill. I like to think that he gave them to his friends. Some of my cases have happy endings in which abused and neglected dogs are found loving homes. But unfortunately, many of my cases end on a more ambiguous note, with puppy mill operators sent right back into the nebulous realms they came from, bound by laws and regulations that are rarely enforced. For every puppy mill operator like Reuben Wee who has been shut down, there are hundreds more who operate with impunity, the beneficiaries of second, third, and fourth chances. Without civilian investigators willing to risk their lives to visit puppy mills and publicly call out their operators, the number of convictions would fall close to zero.

DAVIDA

Bringing Down the Puppy Mill Capital of the East

Lancaster County in southeastern Pennsylvania is surprisingly beautiful, with lush, rolling hills and neatly tended crops. Tiny roads snake their way around picturesque barns and silos built centuries ago. After a storm, wispy mists rise from the scenic ponds that dot the landscape. People drive slowly here, with road signs beseeching drivers to share the road with horse-drawn carriages. This is Amish country.

I've spent so much time in Lancaster County that I know its winding roads by memory. I know the modest Mennonite churches and the creaky one-lane bridges that traverse streams. Yet the beautiful scenery and quaint lifestyle conceal a dark secret: Lancaster County is the puppy mill capital of the east.

In the early 2000s, CAPS was investigating pet stores and building a database of known suppliers. Puppies were flowing into pet stores from traditional midwestern states like Missouri, Iowa, and Minnesota and mega-brokers like the Hunte Corporation. But Pennsylvania was quickly becoming a hotbed, supplying pet stores all across the Eastern Seaboard. Specifically, the breeders were located in Lancaster County. This seemed strange: How could a small population that avoids electricity, vehicles, and other conveniences have the means to export tens of thousands of puppies every year?

Furthermore, anecdotal reports indicated that Amish puppy mills harbored some of the worst conditions of any kennels in the United States.

I took two trips in 2005 to Amish country, once in the winter and then again in spring, to document as much as possible about this little-known corner of the multibillion-dollar puppy industry. In general, the Amish greeted me warmly and spoke perfect English, but when alone they reverted to the German dialect called Pennsylvania Dutch. Their clothing is as plain as their lifestyle, reflecting their values of modesty and humility—the result of seventeenth-century sumptuary laws in Europe of which the Amish founder and namesake, Jakob Ammann, was a strict adherent. Married Amish men maintain stout beards and wear broad-brimmed hats, dark suits, broadfall trousers, suspenders, and shirts fastened with large buttons. Women wear modest dresses made from solid-colored fabric and cover their heads with bonnets at all times, as dictated by 1 Corinthians 11:5–6: "But every woman that prayeth or prophesieth with her head uncovered dishonoureth her head: for that is even all one as if she were shaven."

I did not attempt to go undercover as an Amish man. Even I have limits. Instead, I posed as a journalist writing for the fictional *Commercial Canine*, promoting the dog-breeding industry; it's a cover I usually avoid because a cursory internet search can destroy my story in thirty seconds, but the Amish weren't about to google my LinkedIn profile.

Reports at the time indicated there were roughly three hundred licensed breeders in Lancaster County, along with another six hundred unlicensed facilities that went to extreme lengths to conceal their presence. Activists who visited the area were alleging that puppy mill operators were hammering sharp objects down dogs' throats to scar their vocal cords, preventing them from barking.

Driving onto an Amish property always felt like traveling three centuries into the past. Men with long beards and suspenders would stop their wooden plows drawn by massive draft horses and approach me with the kind of suspicion honed after a lifetime of keeping the modern world at bay. Amish children would gather around me and stare, eyes and mouths agape. I had more to overcome than just puppy millers' basic suspicion of activists. I had to overcome the Amish's basic mistrust of outsiders.

Still, given my cover, I was able to visit nearly a dozen puppy mills a day. The vast majority were run by Amish farmers, with the remainder operated by Mennonites. Both groups are Anabaptist—a Christian movement that emphasizes adult baptism—who insist on wearing plain clothes, although Mennonites allow for more technology, such as washers, tractors, and telephones. Some of the kennels were advertised with large signs, and the owners greeted me warmly. The Amish referred to me as "English" when I visited—the customary way Amish refer to all outsiders. Despite the absence of modern technology, the Amish puppy mills looked very similar to others I had visited in the Midwest. The dogs were typically kept in wire cages with indoor and outdoor sections and runs that had mud-and-snow floorings. Because the Amish don't use electricity, the pens were unheated and many of the water bowls were frozen solid. Unable to use electric shavers, dogs were left ungroomed. Their fur was tangled, dirty, and matted with feces. I saw eye infections and open, bloody wounds.

One of the first kennels I visited was run by Amos Stoltzfus, who was licensed by the USDA to breed dogs. He was working in a barn when I met him, and he didn't look like he had much time for me when I mentioned my magazine, *Commercial Canine*. "It's a magazine for people like you, Amos," I explained.

"Well, I don't read any magazines."

"Right, but see, this isn't for you specifically. It's for the dog breeding industry. There's no publication that exists to represent this industry. People don't realize that breeders like you are professionals, with the best-quality pets money can buy."

Stoltzfus raised his eyebrows. I had tapped into his ego—step one.

"I sell all my puppies already," he said.

"Right, because you no doubt have great breeding stock. But with cooperation among breeders, and more respect from the public for what you do, you could get supplies cheaper and sell puppies for more profit."

Amos smiled. I had tapped into his greed—step two. Just one step left.

"So what do you need from me?" he asked.

"Well, I need to know what you want. Who do you want to sell to? What improvements do you want for your kennel? What kind of breeding stock are you looking for? Let's take a look at your stock and talk all about it."

Stoltzfus looked at his dirty boots and mumbled, "Well, my kennel isn't really all that clean right now."

"Don't worry about that. I've been in the breeding business my whole life. Dirty kennels don't bother me."

Step three—Stoltzfus walked me to his kennel, and I began covertly recording video. I realized why Amos didn't want me there: He had dozens of dogs kept in two small barns. All the dogs lived in raised wire cages, with sawdust on concrete below them that was soaked in urine and feces. The stench of ammonia was overwhelming. Brown cobwebs mixed with fur clung to the undersides of cages, filled with dogs frantically running in circles and into one another as they panted in excitement that someone had come to see them.

I noticed a bichon stick her head out of a dark, plastic whelping box. She had cherry eye, a curable condition in which glands prolapse out from under eyelids and partially block the eyeballs. Her condition appeared untreated, with the glands severely swollen and blood spattering her muzzle below her eyes. Stitches sutured an old wound on the left side of her face. I smiled at everything, complimented Stoltzfus for how good his dogs looked, and didn't feel the slightest pang of guilt for lying to him to gain access to his kennel. Instead, I swallowed anger.

Local law enforcement generally assumes a hands-off approach with the Amish populations. They often vote as a bloc when it comes to issues affecting their everyday lives, such as zoning and livestock regulations. This means district attorneys tend to let the Amish police themselves, even on issues like domestic abuse and child labor.

Still, I decided to document as many puppy mill violations as possible. Even if local prosecutors wouldn't touch the case, we could help the public understand where their pets were coming from. In the spring of 2005, I returned to Lancaster County to revisit the same puppy mills I had visited months earlier to confirm that the violations were still present. Little had changed. The frozen piles of manure inside cages were replaced with wet piles of feces swarming with maggots and flies. The dogs were ungroomed, and their fur remained filthy and matted. Yet these kennels continued to pass their USDA inspections without any reported violations.

Perhaps the most flagrant example of a kennel violating federal law was a USDA-licensed puppy mill owned by a man named David Blank, who lived in a small town called Gap in Lancaster County. Blank owned about thirty dogs of the most popular breeds at the time: miniature pinschers, poodles, pugs, cocker spaniels, shih tzu, bichon frises, Jack Russell terriers, dachshunds, and schnauzers. I visited Blank posing as a journalist, and he gladly gave me a tour of his kennel. With my hidden camera rolling, I documented how dogs huddled inside makeshift wooden boxes to escape snow and rain. Other cages had plastic barrels with doggy doors crudely cut into them. USDA inspectors hadn't bothered to mention these completely inadequate shelters in their reports. Dogs had matted fur and were covered in dirt. Water bowls were filled with solid blocks of ice.

Inside the whelping barn I found breeder dogs living in tiny wire cages. As I looked around, a matted shih tzu cowered in the corner of one cage, shaking and refusing to move while other dogs barked and jumped anxiously. I stopped and focused my attention on an extremely underweight female miniature pinscher who weighed no more than five pounds. When I opened her cage she stumbled toward me, her tiny paws falling through the cage wire. She was black and brown and was missing patches of fur on her upper rear legs, hips, and near her eyes. The tiny dog was clearly desperate to escape the prison in which she spent nearly all her life. Before I could react, she jumped into my arms and burrowed her head in my elbow. The bare patches of skin on her legs were scaly and gray and oozed pus. Her eyelids were swollen about three times their normal size.

I tried placing her back in the cage, but her paws dug into my arms. She hooked her arms around my shoulders and tried to launch herself onto the ground. I hated myself for restraining her, but there was nothing I could do. Gently, I placed her back in her cage. She stared me in the eye fleetingly before retreating into a corner. Later, when Deborah and I reviewed and packaged my footage for law enforcement, we referred to the tiny miniature pinscher as Davida, after her owner, David Blank. When we don't know the names of dogs in the field, we sometimes name them after their kennel operator to keep my hundreds of pages of notes organized. Davida deserved a better name, just as she deserved a family to love and care for her. But the name was also fitting. Davida, like her owner, was the face of the Pennsylvania puppy mill industry. Her swollen eyes, her open wounds, her desperate attempt to flee her own personal hell symbolized everything that is wrong with the industry.

CAPS assembled my notes and footage and sent it to the agency responsible for regulating puppy mills, the Pennsylvania Bureau of Dog Law Enforcement. Unsurprisingly, we never heard back. This was nothing new, as the bureau, like the USDA, was notorious for turning a blind eye to the very abuses it was designed to prevent. If activists wanted to help dogs like Davida, we needed to exert political pressure to change the culture of the bureau from within.

Fortunately, we had a powerful ally in Pennsylvania governor Edward Rendell. Elected in 2003, Rendell, a lifelong dog lover, was one of the few politicians concerned about Pennsylvania's sordid reputation concerning dogs. And he was friendly with businesswoman and philanthropist Marsha Perelman, a longtime animal advocate who moved in powerful circles in Philadelphia. Perelman was on the board of the American Society for the Prevention of Cruelty to Animals (ASPCA) and was determined help Pennsylvania's dogs by exposing the state's puppy mills.

Bob Baker, an investigator at the ASPCA, was aware of my work for CAPS and my extensive travels in Lancaster County. In early 2006 he had an idea: What if Perelman hired me directly to compile evidence against Lancaster County's puppy mills? She could take my footage and bring it directly to Governor Rendell, who had authority over the Pennsylvania Bureau of Dog Law Enforcement. I soon met with Perelman, who explained the governor was ready to clean house at the bureau and replace the industry cronies with true animal advocates.

"Let's do it," I said.

For the first time in my career, I'd been hired to investigate puppy mills by a private citizen. I felt energized knowing that my hard work would not be destined for the bottom of the local district attorney's case file. Chances like this seldom arose.

In May 2006, I dyed and cut my hair and grew a beard, and then visited Lancaster County once again. This time around, I posed as a guy trying to buy puppies; I now had so much experience dealing with breeders that I felt confident I could talk my way into anywhere I needed to go. Over the course of two weeks, I investigated eighteen puppy mills and discovered the very same conditions I had documented a year earlier. Still no changes. Malnourished dogs with matted fur living on cage wire above piles of feces. Moldy kibble. Muddy water. Dogs with open wounds and untreated infections.

Since I had last visited the Amish kennels, their breeding licenses had been renewed by both the USDA and the Pennsylvania Bureau of Dog Law Enforcement. Government inspectors knew violations were present, yet nothing had been done. As I toured the kennels and spoke with the owners, nearly all of whom were Amish or Mennonite, I wondered why they would allow their animals to live in such terrible conditions. They seemed like good people. They had loving families. I wanted to like them. I wanted to think that people who believed in simple living would also believe in simple compassion. But like CC Baird, Reuben Wee, Neal Spies, and the countless other puppy mill operators I'd known, it came down to a simple fact: In this country, dogs are considered livestock. The Amish spoke about their dogs like they spoke about wagons, like other puppy mill operators talked about their trucks. It would be impossible to convince these people to treat their dogs compassionately when they don't see dogs as worthy of compassion.

Breeders counted their dogs by "the head," the same term used for other livestock. As for how long breeders could use their dogs for, they would usually tell me, "I get about seven years out of them before I have to cull." *Cull* was used in the same way as "culling livestock," which meant selling off or killing them. Some breeders attempted to give their old breeding dogs away to rescues, but most preferred to shoot their dogs and bury them on-site. Others sold their dogs at enormous profit at auctions, where rescue groups paid high prices to rescue the dogs while inadvertently lining the pockets of puppy millers.

I submitted my evidence to Perelman just as Governor Rendell was beginning to overhaul the Bureau of Dog Law Enforcement. Within weeks he fired most of the leadership as well as the entire panel who "advised" the bureau—including a notorious puppy mill operator who counted eight hundred dogs in his kennel. Almost overnight, the agency shifted its mission from protecting puppy mills to cracking down on them. Suddenly, inspectors were flagging previously ignored items like matted fur, dirty food bowls, rusty cage wire, and manure piles. Breeders were outraged. At the first of numerous public meetings, three hundred predominantly Amish and Mennonite breeders packed the Farm Show Complex & Expo Center in Harrisburg, arguing that the bureau's regulations posed an undue burden on their business. Yet the bureau, under the leadership of its newly appointed head, Jessie Smith—formerly a deputy state attorney general—did not waver.

Instead of upgrading their facilities to address new requirements for light, temperature, airflow, and exercise, many kennels simply shut down. In October 2007, CAPS sent me once again to Pennsylvania to visit dozens of puppy mills that had not renewed their license. Supposedly they had shut down rather than conform to the new regulations, but I suspected many of them were still operating illegally. I was working with the blessing of Smith, who even asked me to speak to a gathering of the state's dog wardens, who were charged with inspecting and regulating kennels. At a convention center in Hershey, Pennsylvania, I was introduced to the room of inspectors by Smith herself. At twenty-eight, I was the youngest person in the room.

"This is Pete," Smith told them. "And you need to take everything he says seriously. If he reports any violations, you need to investigate."

Some of the wardens smiled and listened attentively, while others looked annoyed—at the new regulations they were required to enforce, at the long hours they would now have to log, at the kid in the camo hat who was telling them how to do their job. I politely explained my background and what I would be doing for the next several weeks, but I didn't care if I pissed off every dog warden in the state if it meant we could shut down even one puppy mill. I made a point of getting cards from the inspectors who seemed most willing to hear me out.

Once again I toured the puppy mills of Lancaster County, but with the promise of cooperation from the dog wardens, I extended my operating zone to counties across the state. By Pennsylvania law, anyone owning more than twenty-six dogs required a state breeder's license. As I suspected, many of the breeders who failed to renew their licenses were clearly still in operation. The signs advertising puppies had been removed, and many of the dog runs were moved to the back of the properties. The kennel operators were on the lookout for inspectors, so I had to convince them I was ready to buy puppies in cash. Amish puppy millers may dress, speak, work, and worship differently from other puppy millers, but they share something in common: greed. My simple plan to uncover unlicensed puppy mills was to ask the property owners if they were still breeding dogs, making it clear I was ready to pay top dollar. Sure enough, the unlicensed breeders were eager to sell to me. This strategy worked repeatedly, enabling me to walk into supposedly defunct breeding kennels.

While conducting research, I noticed that one breeder whom I had visited the previous year, Alvin Zimmerman, had not renewed his license for 2007. When I visited his property again, I heard what appeared to be dozens of dogs barking from inside a barn with small windows lining the walls. Zimmerman was Amish and unmarried, as evidenced by his clean-shaven face. (Customarily, only married Amish men grow beards.) He wore suspenders and a fedora that was too small for his head.

"Are you still breeding dogs?" I asked him. "I'd like to buy some puppies."

Zimmerman mumbled something noncommittal but agreed to

show me a few puppies after I offered to pay in cash. After telling me to stay put, he scurried off to a barn across the property, whereupon I sprinted over to the barn and peered through the window. The Amish don't use electric lighting, so I could only make out an empty, rusted cage with crusty feces piled up beneath it. Deeper inside the musty barn I could hear easily dozens of dogs barking. I hustled back to my car and waited for Zimmerman to return.

He brought me a few cockapoo puppies—a cocker spaniel–poodle crossbreed that was popular at the time. The puppies winced at the sun, as if they hadn't been outside in a very long time. I told Zimmerman I'd come back later with cash. Five minutes later I called one of the dog wardens who had given me his card and explained what I saw. I didn't expect anything to happen, but sure enough, on November 13, the Bureau of Dog Law Enforcement raided Zimmerman's property. Soon after, Jessie Smith put out a press release:

> State dog wardens assisted humane officers in recovering
> 29 dogs from an unlicensed Union County facility as part
> of Governor Edward G. Rendell's effort to crack down on
> unsatisfactory kennels. State dog wardens visited Fairview
> kennel in Lewisburg to investigate a complaint about the
> facility operating without a license Tuesday. The wardens
> found 29 of the 40 dogs were dirty, matted and living in
> unsanitary conditions, including excess fecal matter.

Zimmerman was later charged with operating a kennel without a license and keeping dogs in unsanitary conditions. Twenty-nine of his dogs were rescued by humane officers. I was dumbfounded. In a place routinely derided as the "puppy mill capital of the east," state authorities had raided a facility based solely on my word. Momentum continued to build. CAPS posted video after video of my investigations online as other activist groups joined the fight. In early 2008, an investigator named Bill Smith and his organization, Main Line Animal Rescue, launched an extremely effective billboard campaign against Pennsylvania's puppy mills that caught the eye of Oprah Winfrey. She dispatched a TV crew to shadow Smith as he ventured through kennel country, revealing the squalid conditions in which puppy mill dogs lived. The segment aired on national television and further galvanized the belief that more regulations needed to be passed.

As inspectors stepped up their efforts, puppy mill operators took drastic measures. In July 2008, two kennel owners in Berks County, Pennsylvania, located just north of Lancaster, decided they were fed up with regulations—namely one that required dogs to be treated for fleas. One morning the two men took shotguns and opened fire at their own poodles, shih tzu, and cocker spaniels. More than eighty dogs were massacred in their tiny hutches and dumped in a compost pile. When the bodies were discovered, the public demanded the authorities take action against the breeders. But nothing could be done. Thanks to widespread exemptions for animals considered to be livestock, this was entirely legal. When a regulation as trivial as a flea bath begins to erode a profit margin, something peculiar happens. In the eyes of businessmen, dogs look less like living, breathing creatures and more like cash crops that need to be harvested as cheaply as possible. Corners are cut, regulations are ignored, and when costs are too high, the product is destroyed.

After the massacre, merely revamping the Bureau of Dog Law Enforcement wasn't good enough. Merely getting the dog wardens to do their job wasn't good enough. We needed to pass legislation that shut down the worst puppy mills. But this would require shepherding a bill through the Pennsylvania state legislature—no easy task. In spring 2008, Governor Rendell introduced HB 2525, known as the Pennsylvania Dog Law. Among other items, the bill sought to double the cage size for breeding dogs, require dogs to have access to the outdoors, mandate twenty-four-hour access to water, and make it illegal to keep dogs on wire floorings. In addition, dogs could also no longer be euthanized by gunshot.

The puppy mill industry fought back ravenously, using their lobbyists in Harrisburg to smother the bill with amendments designed to delay a final vote indefinitely. The winds of change were too great. The Pennsylvania House of Representatives overwhelmingly passed the bill 181–17 on September 17, 2008. The Senate passed it shortly after, and Governor Rendell signed the bill into law on October 9. At the signing ceremony, the governor was joined by one of his dogs, a golden retriever named Maggie, who had been rescued from an Amish puppy mill a year earlier.

"We the people of Pennsylvania, we the dog lovers of Pennsylvania, decided that Pennsylvania's time had come to end being called the 'puppy mill of the east.' And we did that," Rendell said. The law worked. Over the next four years, the number of commercial USDA-licensed kennels in Pennsylvania plummeted from around three hundred to just thirty. For most puppy mills, the cost of treating dogs with respect and compassion was simply too high.

Our work is not done in Pennsylvania. In recent years, the number of large-sale kennels has begun to increase again, and there are hundreds of smaller-scale kennels that avoid certain regulations by keeping their breeder population below minimum requirements. Lying and cheating is still rampant in the industry, especially among Amish kennels, which enjoy a hands-off relationship with law enforcement. But activists have continued to maintain pressure on elected officials. In 2017, Pennsylvania governor Tom Wolf signed Libre's Law, named after a dog named Libre who narrowly escaped death after being rescued from a Lancaster County puppy mill. The law updated the existing animal-cruelty statute, substantially increased penalties for violations, and made it easier for prosecutors to pursue felony convictions.

Puppy mills will continue to be a problem in Pennsylvania as long as dogs are bought and sold for profit. I still think about Davida, the dog I met in Lancaster County so many years ago. Her desperate attempts to flee her filthy cage are burned in my mind. I hope that Davida found peace, and I wish I could have done more for her. No dog should be forced into an existence like that, despite how many laws are passed to protect her. A cage is still a cage, no matter how large you make it.

MAGGIE

Shutting Down a Ruthless Breeder

'vc visited hundreds of kennels over my career. Many of them are quite literally mom-and-pop outfits and are not puppy mills in the traditional sense—although the abuse is always present, no matter how small the operation. As I've discovered over my eighteen years investigating everything from kennels to factory farms, combining animals with a profit motive is a recipe for abuse and neglect. When compassion equals diminished margins and basic care equals a competitive disadvantage, dogs are going to suffer.

Some kennel operators are good people in a bad line of work. But every once in a while I come across genuine, real-life Cruella de Vils—people so infatuated with inflicting misery on innocent creatures that there is only one appropriate word to describe them: evil. In April 2008, I met a real-life Cruella in the strange little town of New York Mills, Minnesota. This is the story of one of the most notorious puppy mills in history.

Pick of the Litter Kennels was a commercial, USDA-licensed operation run by a woman named Kathy Bauck. Kathy and her husband, Alan, first began breeding dogs in the early 1980s, selling mainly to pet stores. With the growth of the internet, the Baucks, like many other commercial breeders, boosted their margins by selling directly to consumers. By the late 1990s the kennel had exploded in size, housing nearly nine hundred breeding dogs of practically every breed. In 1996, a veterinarian complained to the Otter Tail County Sheriff's Office that Kathy Bauck was subjecting her dogs to horrendous treatment. According to reports by the vet and three other informants, Kathy—who was not a licensed veterinarian—was conducting her own C-sections without the use of antiseptics and performing her own spays and neuters. Yet more whistle-blowers reported that sick puppies were not provided care and were often left to die in cages and decompose among their still-living littermates. Kathy was also accused of cajoling a vet to sign certificates of veterinary inspection for puppies he had never seen, allowing Kathy to sell massive numbers of sick puppies to unsuspecting consumers.

Inexplicably, nothing happened. Kathy continued to operate with impunity. The USDA renewed her license, and local law enforcement refused to investigate the steady stream of complaints made against her. Fast-forward ten years: A veterinarian named Dr. Dennis Stanford examined a puppy who had been purchased months earlier from Pick of the Litter Kennels. The spaying procedure had been botched and clearly wasn't performed by a vet. Dr. Stanford complained to the sheriff's office, who passed the case on to the Minnesota Board of Veterinary Medicine. The board promptly sent Kathy a cease-and-desist letter for practicing veterinary medicine without a license. Despite this latest second chance in a long line of second chances, Kathy ignored the order.

The drip, drip of complaints continued from former workers. Instead of paying a vet, Bauck was still performing her own spays and neuters, performing her own C-sections, and administering dangerous medications without a license. One worker had even witnessed her kill a puppy by slamming her into a pole. Finally, at long last, the Otter Tail County Sheriff's Office took action. In April 2008,

Kathy Bauck was charged with five counts of practicing veterinary medicine without a license and one count of animal cruelty. But the wheels of justice move slowly—painfully slowly, when it comes to animals—and court dates came and went. Despite the ongoing legal proceedings, Kathy still had her USDA license, and Pick of the Litter Kennels continued to churn at full capacity.

By spring 2008, Kathy was running one of the largest puppy mills in the country, housing some 1,300 dogs and puppies. Through her sources in law enforcement, Deborah Howard with CAPS had heard that Kathy was in the midst of negotiating a plea bargain—one that would likely let her continue breeding and selling dogs. We didn't trust the justice system to put an end to her operation, so CAPS sent me undercover in April to document every violation in her puppy mill. We needed firm video evidence if we had any chance of shutting her down for good.

But this wasn't a normal undercover operation. Most kennels or factory farms I target don't know I'm coming—or even that they're being targeted by activist groups. In this case, Kathy was aware that her employees had been snitching on her, and she realized she'd been targeted by undercover investigators before. She was on high alert.

I arrived in New York Mills in early April 2008. It's a frostbitten place of about 1,200 people eighty miles southeast of Fargo, North Dakota. In winter the temperatures rarely peak above freezing and often linger close to zero. Towns like New York Mills must be dragged kicking and screaming into spring, with frigid temperatures remaining well into April and May. "You'll feel at home here" is the town's official motto, although the still-frozen tundra did little to remind me of sunny North Carolina. On a cold, wet morning I arrived in the town of Wadena, above fifteen minutes southeast of New York Mills, in search of a place to live. As with most of my cases, I avoided living too close to my target. Kathy would be on the lookout for activists.

Before I applied for a job at Pick of the Litter, I needed to carefully construct my backstory. Prep work is paramount to success. I found a trailer park where the owner, a shifty man with anxious eyes, was all too happy to show me his cheapest place—the bottom story of a small duplex house in the park, with no working heat and spotty carpeting. When I inspected the apartment, murky brown water was dripping into the kitchen from the ceiling. "The guy upstairs is taking a shower," the landlord explained. "But don't worry—he only showers once per week."

I handed over a month's rent in cash and moved in that day.

After visiting the local DMV and acquiring a Minnesota driver's license and new plates, I went to work. First, I needed to know everything about Kathy—her temperament, her sense of humor, her quirks. As I knew nothing at this point, I broke one of my basic rules: I reached out to a former employee of Kathy's who had informed law enforcement about her cruelty toward animals. Normally I don't want anyone besides Deborah at CAPS knowing where I am working, but this case was requiring new rules and new tactics.

I called the former employee, Monica, and explained in vague terms that I was working with CAPS to help bring down Pick of the Litter Kennels. To my relief, she instantly told me everything I needed to know. Monica described Kathy as an unpredictable bully who needed to believe she had control over her employees. She often hired people who couldn't get jobs anywhere else because they'd been busted for using heroin or meth.

"She really likes to lord over kids who are down on their luck," Monica told me. "Now, some people are good Christians and truly want to help the neediest, most desperate people. But Kathy? She just wants someone pathetic to kick around."

I asked Monica to promise not to tell anyone about our conversation. Despite her assurances, I had trouble sleeping that night. I didn't know anything about Monica. People talk, and information travels fast in small towns. Was she trustworthy?

I drove to Pick of the Litter Kennels the following morning. Armed with Monica's information, I was ready to talk myself into a job. Kathy lived on the property, her modest house flanked by several barns and dozens of caged dog runs. I parked next to a pen containing huskies. They gazed at me with their brilliant blue eyes, panting and pacing the length of the pen as I approached the house. Then I passed the hulking mastiffs, their booming barks echoing off the barn walls. I saw lean German shepherds and fat Labradors, Yorkshire terriers, Jack Russells, Chihuahuas, cocker spaniels, miniature schnauzers, shih tzu, dachshunds, pugs, Shiba Inus, cairn terriers, Pekingese, poodles, Maltese, and bichons.

The sound was deafening. The stench was overwhelming. It was a dog warehouse. Almost a thousand dogs, and hundreds of puppies, were crammed into concrete pens and wire cages. Dogs spun in circles barking, clawed at cage wire, and ran through doggy doors from indoor cages to outdoor cages in frantic attempts to figure out why everyone else was barking. The kennel was a maze of buildings. Everywhere I looked, I saw rows of dog cages elevated over piles of manure swarming with flies. In front of it all, at the end of the driveway, were neatly manicured flower beds that provided splashes of color before the chaotic scene before me.

Kathy Bauck emerged from one of the barns and approached me. Having worked with dogs for so long, I invariably compare every human I meet with a dog breed. Kathy looked like a bulldog: middle-aged and heavyset with a muscular frame and a weathered face fixed in a permanent scowl. Her long blond hair was pulled back into a ponytail, her lower lip stuck out in defiance, and her oddly small eyes peered out at me from behind her glasses.

"What do you want?" she shouted.

I looked down at the ground and hunched my shoulders. "Is this Pick of the Litter Kennels?" I asked meekly. "I'm looking for work."

Kathy sized me up and launched a volley of questions: *What's your name? Where're you from? How'd you find me? Why do you want to work at a kennel?* I explained I was in the area following a girl, but it hadn't worked out. I didn't have money to leave town. I needed to work. I kept my hands in my pockets and my eyes on the ground, occasionally glancing up at her.

"I pay minimum wage," Kathy said skeptically. "You can work construction for double that. What's so special about this place?"

"That kind of work . . . it really isn't for me . . . ," I said, trailing off. I didn't pretend to have experience working in a kennel. I needed her to think I was young and dumb with a lot of baggage—maybe even a felony conviction or two. I needed her to think I was so desperate I'd do and put up with nearly anything.

"I don't know much about dogs, but I promise I can learn." I shuffled my feet and made eye contact with her for the first time. "Please."

That seemed to work. She began to brag about how big her kennel was, how many dogs she bred, how many stores depended on her, how much money she made. "No one can do what I can do. I'm not afraid to admit that," she said.

"I believe it, ma'am."

"You will eat the fruit of your labor. Blessings and prosperity will be yours." She narrowed her eyes. "You know where that's from?"

In the back of my mind, I quietly thanked my parents: Years of Catholic school were paying off. "Yes, ma'am. That's the Bible."

In between Bible verses she ranted about animal rights activists and the DA who was prosecuting her. She claimed she had done nothing wrong and that all her dogs were incredibly happy to be living with her. Then she gave me the tour of her kennel. She showed the whelping barn for the large-breed dogs. The floors had been gutted and replaced with concrete. Dim heat lamps cloaked in cobwebs dangled from the ceiling. The air reeked of ammonia and manure. Arranged in rows throughout the barn were the whelping pens. There were puppies everywhere. I lost count of the breeds. Weeks-old puppies yipped and scampered about in a row of wire cages, their tiny feet slipping through the cage wire.

"You're in luck," Kathy told me. "I need some help around the kennel. You'll be on probation until I know you're not some filthy activist. The work is hard and dirty and the hours are long. You'll get minimum wage, and don't ask me for a raise. You also don't tell nobody you work here. If someone important keeps asking, you tell them you work at a farm. If they ask what kinda animals you work with, you tell them, 'Dogs.' If they ask how many dogs you work with, you answer, 'Too many.' If they ask how much poop you clean up, you tell them, 'Too much.' You all right with all that?"

"Yes, ma'am. I'm just glad to get back on my feet. That sounds great."

I called Deborah when I got back to my apartment. She was over the moon: Kathy Bauck was her number-one target, and she had been trying for years to place an activist undercover at her kennel.

But Kathy wasn't ready to trust me. She had spent the night hatching a plan to determine whether I was telling the truth. When I arrived at the kennel in the morning, she asked the same questions again to see if my answers changed: *Where're you from? How'd you find me? Why do you want to work at a kennel?* She asked if I was working for the district attorney or for an animal rights group. She came right up to my face and peered at me with her head cocked like an inquisitive parrot.

"I'm not here to cause you any problems, Mrs. Kathy," I said. "I'm not one of those crazy animal people. I just want to work."

That seemed to satisfy her for the moment, but that was only the first salvo in an endless sequence of character tests. My first day on the job, Kathy had me groom dogs with another employee named Donna, a tall, lean, heavily tattooed woman with flowing blond hair. She wasn't much for small talk, so we mainly sat in silence brushing and washing the small-breed dogs. Then, abruptly, Donna recited the same questions Kathy had: *Where're you from? How'd you find this kennel? Why do you want to work here?* She rattled them off in a monotone voice and avoided making eye contact. I assumed Kathy would later compare my answers to make sure my story stayed the same, probably something she picked up from *CSI: Miami*.

Later in the day, Kathy set me up to work with her daughter, Corinne. Corinne was about my age, heavyset, with wavy black hair, fire truck–red fingernails, and a bubbly personality. She brought me to a building that looked as though two mobile homes had been rammed together. Along the edges of the room were large-breed puppies kept in wire cages suspended over concrete. As Corinne and I groomed the yellow Labs and poodles, their littermates barked so loud we could barely hold a conversation.

"So . . . ," Corinne asked me awkwardly. "Where you from? How'd you find our kennel?" I almost laughed out loud but instead softly answered the questions, and then Corinne threw me a curveball: "Well, let me know if you need help settling in. Like where to maybe buy vegetarian food? It's hard around here. . . ."

Corinne gazed at me knowingly, as if expecting me to reveal my secret animal rights agenda. Corinne must have watched the same terrible network TV cop shows as her mother. I was vegan, of course, but Corinne would have to work harder than that to trip me up.

"Like never meat eat at all?" I said incredulously. "I could never do that. Hell no. I love bacon and steak."

Corinne laughed nervously. "Well, I'm a vegetarian. It's pretty easy, actually. I mean, I occasionally eat chicken. And pork. Oh, and definitely burgers. But I'm mostly vegetarian."

It was best not to inform Corinne what vegetarian meant, so I nodded, changed the subject, and asked what she liked to do in her spare time. She immediately began talking about her favorite movies, her friends, her family. She was in the process of a messy divorce and was having a hard time. She hated living in a small town and wanted to move to the big city. Within an hour I had heard her entire life story. I enjoyed talking with Corinne. She was kinder than her mother. I hoped she wouldn't be dragged down with Kathy at the end.

Soon I was working all around the kennel. People often suspect that undercover work means special gadgets and secret hiding places, like scenes from a James Bond movie. Real undercover work is a lot less sexy. There is a time and place for hidden cameras and micro-phones, but most of the job is following instructions and working hard. Instead of driving my Aston Martin to fancy cocktail parties, I spent my days at Pick of the Litter Kennels cleaning up poop. I picked dogs up and put them down. I fixed broken pens. I groomed dogs and gave them baths. I observed everything. For long stretches of time, I didn't even record—I kept my head down and gained the trust of my employer.

It was all worth it. I soaked in as much information about the puppy mill as possible. I learned the layout of the barns and the pens, where every breed was located, where everything was kept. For my first week, my number-one task was to make myself indispensable. I needed Kathy to not just trust me but to rely on me.

This turned out to be the easiest part of the case. As in most of my undercover cases, simply being competent goes a long way. Over the next few days I met the rest of the staff at Pick of the Litter Kennels. I met Larry, a hardworking guy about my age who had climbed his way out of several levels of hell to overcome a meth addiction. Then there was Bill, a tall, wiry fifty-year-old who talked slow, moved even slower, and would sooner jump off a cliff than ask anyone for help. I met Kathy's husband, Alan, who was the spitting image of Paul Bun-yan. He was towering, thick, bearded, and silent, and I was lucky to get a grunt or two out of him. From what I could tell, his only job was to take his .22 rifle and shoot sick dogs whom Kathy deemed too expensive to treat.

There was a young couple who showed up when they weren't on

meth or downers—Adam was skinny and tattooed; Diane talked a mile a minute and couldn't sit still for more than a few seconds. Both had sores on their faces and sunken eyes. Kathy knew they only showed up to make enough money to score, but she didn't care. Many of the other workers were in various stages of addiction or recovery, and it dawned on me why Kathy sought out this demographic. She paid them minimum wage—but she was the only employer in town who would take a chance on them. No prosecutor would ever rely on two junkies like Adam and Diane as their star witnesses.

There was a lot Kathy needed her employees to keep quiet about. Animal Welfare Act violations were everywhere, and I noted them diligently in my reports. Wooden and plastic walls of the dog enclosures were scratched and worn. Ammonia and other overwhelming odors were omnipresent in the whelping barn. Feces stains covered the enclosure walls. Months of waste and ice were piled below nearly all the outdoor cages. Plastic feeders were covered in mold and manure stains. I spotted dozens more every single day.

But violations like these are common at puppy mills, especially large ones. What truly set Pick of the Litter Kennels apart were the criminal violations. I witnessed Kathy continuing to practice veterinary medicine without a license, but this was only the beginning. On April 22, barely a week into the case, I spotted a female American bulldog covered in blood. I determined that a male in a nearby pen had attacked her through the cage wire, which is common when dogs are thrown together in stressful conditions with no exercise. One of her paws was mangled and bloody. She held it up in the air, unable to put weight on it. On one cheek was a five-inch gash. The bulldog wagged her tail and limped over to me when I greeted her. I immediately reported the situation to Kathy, who looked at me strangely and said not to bother with it.

The wound became infected the following day. When I mentioned this to Kathy, she explained: "All you have to do is put a little Clorox water on it." Apparently this was how she treated many open wounds. As an undercover investigator, I do my job at the kennel like any other employee—with the exception of my rolling camera. But I wasn't about to pour bleach on a wounded dog. For the next several days I made the bulldog as comfortable as possible and cleaned the wound, all while documenting Kathy's refusal to seek veterinary care. To my relief, the dog made a slow recovery.

But other animals weren't so lucky. There was a Pekingese, a squat, poofy little thing who suddenly began experiencing seizures. Instead of calling a vet, Kathy had a worker place the dog in a concrete pen by himself. The next day the Pekingese was dead. An English springer spaniel, nursing a litter of puppies, became emaciated and her nose started running constantly. She produced less milk, and her puppies weakened and began dying off. The remedy? A treatment of sugar syrup. A pug had an infected eye that became so swollen it was twice the size of the other eye. The condition—which is easily treatable by a veterinarian—worsened over two weeks as Kathy refused to treat her. When the dog was so weak she could barely stand, Alan shot her. Often, Kathy would deliver puppies with her unsanitary hands. Every day there were a dozen more violations—all of which I filmed and memorialized in my notes. Kathy had so many dogs that she figured it was cheaper to let them fend for themselves or die.

Kathy was also cropping puppies' ears and tails—serious operations that by law require a licensed vet to perform. She often botched the procedure, leaving puppies covered in blood and yelping from pain. Perhaps most shocking, Kathy "dipped" her dogs by dunking them in a trough filled with Prolate/Lintox-HD, a chemical formulated to keep ticks and sarcoptic mange mites off cattle. The chemical is cheap but extremely abrasive and dangerous to use on small companion animals, yet Kathy still routinely submerged puppies and pregnant mothers in it. She even dipped dogs with open wounds. Once, she ordered a severely emaciated English mastiff to be dunked in the tank even though he could barely walk. A week later the mastiff had lost a great deal of weight and his elbows had become swollen and bloody. Soon after I found him seizing in his pen. I kneeled down next to him and rubbed his belly, trying to calm him. His heart was nearly beating out of his chest. Kathy left him alone for hours as he seized, blood bubbling from his mouth, before finally having Alan shoot him with his rifle.

Kathy didn't bother to name her dogs, but strangely she decided to call one particular English bulldog Maggie. Like all bulldogs, Maggie suffered from serious genetic issues, from respiratory problems to hip dysplasia to an inability to breed without artificial insemination. Bulldogs are perhaps the most overbred dog on earth. Their stunted muzzles, bred relentlessly shorter over generations, make breathing difficult, and their overlarge heads, while adorable, mean that 80 percent of English bulldogs must be delivered by C-section. Maggie suffered from all the classic bulldog problems in addition to a horrendous skin problem that left painful sores all over her body. Patches of her fur were missing, revealing gray, scaly skin.

When I alerted Kathy several times to Maggie's worsening condition she finally agreed to move her out of the whelping barn. Kathy figured Maggie was allergic to the wood shavings that covered the ground. Yet she continued to suffer and quickly began losing weight. Soon her ears became swollen and sticky—the hallmark signs of a yeast infection. While painful, yeast infections are very treatable with medication. However, instead of calling a veterinarian, Kathy fed Maggie raw eggs. This treatment did not work. Maggie grew so emaciated she could barely walk. When I continued to press Kathy about Maggie's condition, she explained that it cost too much to treat individual dogs.

The case was coming together extremely quickly. Whatever

apprehensions Kathy had about me vanished. She had no issue flaunting her criminal violations in my presence; she seemed to take joy in hurting dogs and being seen hurting dogs. I was desperate to wrap the case up. Every day the investigation stretched out, more and more dogs were being hurt and killed. But we needed enough footage to prove that Kathy wasn't just occasionally torturing her dogs—she was doing it all the time. That meant staying on the case for a few weeks longer.

Then, everything nearly fell apart. While working in the whelping barn, Kathy stormed up to me, her mouth twisted with rage. She reached out her hand and rubbed her fingers over my face.

"I just heard something unsettling, Pete," she said, rubbing my nose and then my forehead. "Word around town is that Monica says I've hired an undercover investigator from CAPS to work in my kennel." Her thumbs lingered on my eyeballs for a moment, and then she released me. "Is that you?"

Monica had blabbed to someone. *And this is why you can't trust informants*, I thought dimly. I took a moment to compose myself, knowing I'd have to tap into some weapons-grade bullshit to escape this one. I looked Kathy in the eye and said, "Mrs. Kathy, I don't know who Monica is. I've never heard of CAPS. If you have a problem here, it's not with me. I would never do anything to hurt you."

Kathy's expression softened. She felt my face one more time. "Don't be alarmed, Pete. This allows me to read your thoughts through the Lord." I tensed as her fingers passed over my eyeballs, worried that she and the Lord might try to gouge them out. She let me go. "I believe you," she said. That was that.

I had to wrap this case up, pronto. During my lunch break I called Deborah, who immediately got me in touch with her contact at the Otter Tail County Sheriff's Office. As is standard procedure in my undercover cases, Deborah had already alerted law enforcement about my work. She had to be careful to impart only the information the sheriff's office needed to know or she risked compromising my status. If she said too much, or if she began taking direction from a member of law enforcement, by law I would become an official agent of the state, which would shackle me to an onerous set of rules—for one, having to inform Kathy and her employees that their criminal actions could be used against them in court. Instead, I occupied a nebulous area wherein the sheriff's office knew what I was doing, received the video footage and case notes I compiled, but provided no direction. One slip-up from either side could compromise my status at Pick of the Litter Kennels and destroy the case. If I wasn't careful, it also meant I could be held criminally responsible as an accessory to a crime.

After three weeks on the case I compiled the evidence I had assembled and spoke with Detective Keith Van Dyke. Van Dyke was middle-aged and clean-cut. He took notes on everything I said, made no small talk, and offered no sign of emotion about the case. He was all business, and that's how I preferred it. I passed along the footage of Kathy dunking dogs in disinfectant, cropping ears and tails, and performing other illegal operations. I passed along footage of sick dogs who were explicitly denied medical care by Kathy on camera. I passed along evidence of Kathy and Alan hiding illegal medications when a USDA inspector toured the facility and hastily installing rubber mats that prevented puppies' feet from falling through cage wire, which are required at all times by law. ("The minute she leaves, we pull 'em up!" Kathy bragged on camera.)

Van Dyke understood the risks involved in my investigation. He let me do all the talking, only saying "thank you" at the end of our meetings. He provided no direction, no advice, no suggestions—nothing that could be twisted by a defense attorney into official instructions. This also meant that he could not tell me when to stop working at Pick of the Litter Kennels; it was up to me to decide when we had enough evidence.

By my last days on the job, Kathy had reached Nixon-level stages of paranoia—repeatedly questioning all her employees, even long-term ones, about whether they were undercover investigators. She muttered to herself, complaining about how the government was out to get her. It was around this time that her lawyer negotiated a deal for her previous months-long court battle: She would plead guilty to one count of practicing veterinary medicine without a license, but the animal cruelty charge would be dropped. Kathy would spend nights in jail for a short time but would be allowed to work at the kennel during the day. She would keep both her USDA and her Minnesota breeding licenses. Despite torturing animals with botched surgeries and killing at least one dog by smashing her against a pole, she could keep her licenses and continue working. Kathy, true to form, considered this the height of injustice.

I was determined to make sure Kathy Bauck didn't get away with abusing animals again. Because Van Dyke couldn't tell me when to stop working, I kept plugging away, gaining more and more footage. That is, until Kathy took me aside with an unorthodox request.

"Pete," she told me. "This weekend I want you to take Corinne out to the lake. The divorce has been hard on her and it's time she moved on. Take my trailer. It'll be just the two of you, all weekend." She stared at me with her bulldog eyes in a way that suggested this wasn't a request—she would take a pass to mean I was plotting against her.

"Why, sure thing, ma'am! I'd love to!" I said.

Getting romantically involved with the daughter of the target of an undercover investigation: very bad. I spent the next seventy-two hours agonizing over how to get out of it. Fortunately, I was spared. When I returned home from work on Thursday, I had a message on my voicemail Van Dyke's familiar drawl crackled through the speaker: "Please be advised, the sheriff's office is planning to execute a search warrant on Pick of the Litter Kennels." In other words: *Get the hell out.* It was divine intervention, courtesy of the Otter Tail County Sheriff's Office. I packed my bags and called Van Dyke to let him know I was skipping town. "Yup, okay," he said flatly—as always, not betraying any hint of emotion.

While I was happy to leave the kennel for good, my mind wandered to Maggie, who was still wasting away in her pen. Kathy had all but forgotten about her. She barely sniffed at the food I brought her, and her yeast infection had grown worse. She would likely be dead within a week or two.

"Detective," I said. "I don't know when you are planning to raid the kennel, and I know you can't tell me. But there's a dog who is really sick. She's an English bulldog named Maggie." I explained Maggie's medical problems, and Van Dyke listened politely as he always did.

"Thank you for letting me know," he said, and that was that. By five thirty the next morning, I was putting as much distance between me and New York Mills, Minnesota, as humanly possible.

I didn't expect to ever return to that frigid little town, but a year later I was back. Kathy Bauck was standing trial as a result of the evidence I acquired. I was confident: My notes were backed up with time-stamped footage and on-camera confessions. I could easily prove that animal welfare violations were present at Kathy's kennel, that they were common, and that Kathy participated in the abuse regularly. In all my undercover work, whenever I deliver evidence to law enforcement, I deliver an airtight case. As stubborn as Kathy was, I assumed she would cut some sort of deal to give up her business and avoid jail time.

She didn't. In March 2009, I was in the Otter Tail County district attorney's office preparing my testimony. The prosecuting attorney was a young, confident woman named Heather Brandborg. In total, nine charges were filed, four of which were felonies. While some of the counts were for general animal abuse, I was pleased that the felony charges mentioned specific animals, namely the pug with the infected eye whom Kathy refused to treat and eventually killed, and the English mastiff who was left alone seizing in a pool of his own blood.

On the day of the trial I sat on a bench inside the small stone courthouse wearing my customary ball cap and sunglasses to avoid having my photograph published. Then I saw Kathy. Her bulldog eyes noticed me immediately and she veered toward my bench. "I want you to know that I forgive you," she said, and walked away. Despite the mountain of evidence against her, despite the impending felony charges, she truly believed she was innocent.

The trial went smoothly. Brandborg handled the case professionally and efficiently. I calmly explained my background to the jury and explained everything I witnessed. For the most part, however, I let the video footage speak for itself. The jury didn't need me to explain just how malevolent Kathy was.

Bauck's defense attorney was a curious man named Zenas Baer. Tall and pale with graying hair, he was perhaps best known for flooding the airwaves of Minnesota and South Dakota with ads touting his expertise in "circumcision litigation." Baer had filed roughly two dozen lawsuits against doctors and hospitals that perform circumcision, claiming the procedure is an "affront on manhood." He questioned me aggressively, focusing on how I had lied about my background to get a job at Pick of the Litter Kennels. He insinuated I was therefore lying about everything else. It's a common tactic defense attorneys use against me, but I parried his questions by referring back to the footage. Finally, Baer resorted to questioning my CAPS expense reports, asking me if I could possibly explain why I had eaten at Starbucks on the thirteenth, and why I ate at Subway a day later.

I told him I could explain. "I was hungry," I said.

And with that, Zenas Baer rested his case.

The charges were ultimately reduced to two felonies and four misdemeanors, and the jury convicted Kathy Bauck on the latter.

The jury deemed that the dogs at Kathy's puppy mill were livestock, not companion animals, and therefore not subject to felony-level cruelty statutes. In the end, Kathy was sentenced for just one misdemeanor—animal torture—for ignoring the seizing mastiff. For that crime, Kathy was sentenced to ninety days in jail. She ended up serving twenty. Despite the professionalism of the sheriff's office and the prosecutor's office, despite the horrendous crimes I documented on camera for six weeks, Kathy's punishment was barely three weeks in jail and a $500 fine.

But CAPS was ready for this outcome. Deborah and her team maintained constant pressure on the USDA. In the face of a criminal conviction and withering press coverage, the agency eventually moved to terminate Kathy Bauck's license. After a lengthy court battle, the decision was upheld in August 2010. Soon after, she lost her USDA license and was required to sell or donate all but six of her dogs—a far cry from the thousand-plus she once owned.

When I think back to the Bauck case, I inevitably think about Maggie the English bulldog. I never did find out what happened to her, or to any of the other dogs whom Kathy was required to give away. I like to think Maggie recovered and found a forever home.

For me, the ending was bittersweet. We managed to shut down one of the largest and most horrific puppy mills in the country, but it took monumental effort by CAPS, whistle-blowers, activists, former employees, veterinarians, law enforcement agencies, and media outlets—an army that cannot be amassed for every single case. It shouldn't be this hard to help dogs like Maggie.

EMMA

The Reality of So-Called Mom-and-Pop Kennels

As an animal lover, my instinct is to rescue every dog I see when I'm undercover at a puppy mill. I want to bust out of there like Rambo, a yellow Lab under one arm and a poodle under the other. Cases seldom work like that. I have to resist the temptation to free individual dogs, which risks compromising the broader investigation. My success depends entirely on how effectively I navigate the miles of red tape put up to shield the puppy mill industry from oversight—a process that can take months and years. But every once in a while I'm able to help a dog I encounter in the field. This is the story of a very special Chihuahua named Emma, who reminded me why I got into this line of work in the first place. Her story also reveals that even the most innocent-seeming kennels can hide horrendous abuse.

During the summer of 2018, I was conducting a whirlwind investigation of pet stores in the New York metro area for CAPS. A state law that had taken effect two years earlier required stores to buy from only class A dealers—meaning places that actually breed dogs, not merely buy and resell them. Stores could no longer buy from class B dealers, such as the Hunte Corporation or CC Baird, who stockpile

COURTESY OF THE COMPANION ANIMAL PROTECTION SOCIETY

Emma is a brave (and tiny) example of what happens to dogs when the system fails to protect them and the rescue community comes together to save them. Emma is resilient, loving, and very fortunate.

dogs by the thousands and where I and other activists have witnessed ghastly abuse. My job was to learn the names of these breeders and discover who the big players were in one of the largest pet markets in the country. Then I'd investigate them one by one.

The plan was straightforward: I'd walk into each store and express interest in buying a puppy before casually asking questions like, "Who are your suppliers? Are they USDA licensed? Have they received any violations in the past five years?" In my experience, pet store employees either don't know the origins of their dogs, or they lie about them. The most common lie is that the puppies are all "raised in the home, not cages." Every commercial breeder I've visited keeps puppies in raised cages and pens called whelping barns. Pet store employees may even offer photographs of "happy" puppies playing in grassy lawns with their breeders; these are about as realistic as the stock photos that come in department store picture frames. Perhaps my favorite lie is that puppies mainly come from the Midwest because there is so much space for them to run around. In reality, most puppies come from the Midwest because these states have lax animal cruelty laws and cheap farmland to build large-scale dog enclosures. Commercial breeders keep their dogs in cages and pens, and they are never allowed to roam free. I have never encountered a single exception to this in my entire career.

Some of the New York stores agreed to show me the paperwork; others sensed I was an investigator and found creative reasons to pass. I visited about eighty stores before word got around about what I was doing—pet stores in New York talk to one another, and they are on a constant lookout for activists. By September, my photograph was probably in every pet store back office from Staten Island to City Island— but not before I acquired a treasure trove of supplier information.

The most curious name that kept popping up was Wanda's Li'l Stars, owned by Wanda and Jerry Johnson and located in the middle of Nebraska. I first heard the name at American Dog Club in Bay Shore, New York—a massive store that kept their dogs inside glass-lined walls, like some freakish puppy aquarium. Before they realized who I was, the employees at American Dog Club showed me the website for Wanda's Li'l Stars. It looked like it had been designed in the 1990s and featured grainy pictures of Chihuahuas and huskies. The landing page read:

> We are not by any stretch of the imagination a breeder who doesn't care about their dogs. Every dog has the attention and the love that it deserves every day. We welcome you to come and visit the dogs and the kennels at any time that you like in order to satisfy your own curiosity and to ensure that the puppy that you take home is from a loving and nurturing environment.

The staff at American Dog Club assured me that Wanda's Li'l Stars was not a puppy mill. "They raise their puppies in their home," they insisted like every other store, much like a used-car salesman purring that the Chevy you're buying was owned by a little old lady who drove only to church. But Wanda's Li'l Stars did in fact seem like a genuine mom-and-pop operation. Was it possible this breeder was different from all the others?

Shortly thereafter I arrived in Doniphan, Nebraska, about a two-hour drive west of Omaha. Dusty and barren, Doniphan is the kind of place you envision storm chasers tearing through in pursuit of F5 tornadoes. Wanda's Li'l Stars was directly off I-80, which bisects Nebraska and offers some of the flattest landscape I've ever seen. I pulled off exit 318, and a moment later I was gliding down the Johnsons' driveway, flanked by neatly groomed trees and flower beds. Puppy mills that purport to be happy family-run operations often invite visitors to tour their kennel—but not without an appointment, which gives them time to clean up their act and put on a good show. By showing up unannounced, I get a good understanding of how the dogs are treated when no one is watching.

At first glance Wanda's Li'l Stars seemed legitimate. Huskies pranced in spacious, surprisingly clean dog runs. In back I saw a collection of small, orderly sheds attached to runs layered with rubber mats. Tiny, multicolored Chihuahuas barked at me as they ran in circles. At most of the kennels I visit, the USDA violations ring up in my head like a pinball machine. Rusted cage wire here, feces-stained concrete there, matted fur here, *ding, ding, ding*—but Wanda's Li'l Stars was better. The runs were well maintained; the enclosures were apparently cleaned daily. "At Wanda's Li'l Stars, we don't have pets—we have friends," the website had read.

I walked back to the house, knocked on the glass back door, and peered inside. An elderly man, napping on the couch, woke with a start. I smiled apologetically. He smiled back, labored to his feet, and waved me inside.

"Hi there!" he said, shaking my hand. "Jerry Johnson." Jerry was tall, tanned, and lean with an honest smile. He didn't seem concerned that I had arrived unannounced, which was a good sign.

"I'm Pete," I replied. A husky padded over and nuzzled me. Jerry was relentlessly polite, ushering me to his living room and offering me a coke. I wanted to like Jerry; he seemed like a kindly old man who raised puppies in his home. But I also realized that even if I found violations or overt signs of abuse, local law enforcement would take one look at this good-natured grandpa and then apologize for wasting his time.

Jerry smiled sweetly as I explained I was looking to buy a puppy. "Why, sure," he said. "Come with me." He brought me to an air-conditioned bedroom, which served as the whelping area for new-borns. Tiny Chihuahua puppies were rolling around inside an enclosure layered with freshly laundered towels. One puppy jumped to his feet and pressed his paws up against the cage wire, trying to reach us. Jerry laughed and tickled the puppy's belly. If Disney made a movie about where puppies came from, it would look something like this.

And then I looked across the room. A mother Chihuahua was curled up in the corner nursing two puppies. She was trembling and gaunt. One of her puppies was a healthy pink, but the other was smaller and a purplish gray.

"That one ain't gonna make it," Jerry said, gesturing to the smaller puppy. "Sometimes that happens."

"Can I see her?"

He plucked the puppy out of her cage and placed her in my hands. Her skin was cold and hard.

"Do you give them medicine when this happens? Or call a vet?" I asked.

Jerry shrugged. "My wife just tries to hand-feed them."

I put the puppy back in the pen, and that's when I got a closer look at the mother. Her tongue was hanging out the side of her mouth. She had no lower jaw.

Jerry sensed my shock and sighed. "She had a broken jaw somewhere. I don't know whether they got to fighting out there in the kennel or what. She does fine—I mean, how she eats I don't know. But she does."

"But you still breed her?" I asked. Jerry just shrugged again. She was clearly too weak to be breeding and nursing puppies.

"So what kind of puppy are you looking for?" Jerry asked, eager to change the subject.

Wanda's Li'l Stars was ultimately a business and their product was dogs. They had a vested interest in keeping most of their puppies healthy, but that mentality clearly did not extend to the older dogs used for breeding. Like any other puppy mill, the mothers were provided the bare minimum of care and were likely disposed of when they became too weak.

"Actually, I'm interested in an older dog," I said. "Do you have any breeders that you wouldn't mind parting with?"

"Wanda has a Chihuahua who's about three or four and just won't breed. Don't know why."

Jerry brought me to the backyard, where the adult Chihuahuas used for breeding were kept. "This is Emma," he said, pointing to the smallest dog in the enclosure. She was a tiny thing with white and brown fur, big bat-like ears, spindly legs, and a pudgy body—like a potato with four matchsticks sticking out. Emma's eyes were large and watery and pointed in slightly different directions. I reached out to her and she scampered off to hide in the corner of the enclosure. Jerry reached in and scooped her up.

"She might have a few issues," Jerry said mildly, placing Emma in my hands. "But she's up to date with her shots and all that."

Emma was trembling and squirming and trying with all her might to escape my grip. She recoiled when I touched her lips. Jerry looked at me and then he looked away, hands stuffed in his pockets. I gently pushed her lips back.

Emma's remaining teeth were brown and horrendously decayed, layered in tartar. Her gums were inflamed and recessed. There was more brown in her mouth than pink or white. These were the "issues" Jerry mentioned. I've seen teeth like these in very old dogs, but never a three-year-old Chihuahua. I couldn't imagine the kind of pain she was in.

"Government inspectors don't really mess with you much, do they?" I said as I inspected Emma's mouth.

"Nah, they're all right. The Nebraska state inspector is a nice guy, Doug. We're friends with him. They send a dentist once a year or so, too. He doesn't give us much grief."

Yeah, no shit he doesn't, I thought, feeling one of Emma's rotten teeth moving in its socket.

"We have some other dogs, over here . . . ," Jerry continued, strolling toward the huskies.

"How much?" I said, not taking my eyes from Emma.

"For her? How about a hundred?"

"I'll take her."

I had to drive more than an hour to get to the nearest town where I could buy a doggy crate, a harness, and some wet canned dog food. I didn't want Emma biting into hard kibble with her rotten teeth. When I arrived back at the kennel, Wanda Johnson had returned to the house. She was as welcoming as her husband, and brought Emma out to my car. Wanda was a short, sturdy woman with a shock of gray hair and a lined face. I handed over five twenties and we shook hands. When I held Emma, she pushed her tiny paws into my chest, craning her head away from me and shaking in fear. I gently set her into the crate I had bought and she promptly fell asleep.

I made small talk with the Johnsons. They weren't bad people. Many of the thousands of kennels in America are probably owned by people like Wanda and Jerry. They provided sufficient food and shelter for their dogs. They didn't hit them. Yet as quaint as Wanda's Li'l Stars looked, it was still a puppy mill. It was a place where a dog could lose her jaw and still be forced to breed puppies. It was a place where a little Chihuahua could go her entire life without basic dental care—not because Wanda and Jerry were cruel but because they wanted to save money.

I said goodbye to the Johnsons and turned onto I-80. I looked over at Emma. Her eyes were heavy and sad, and she was panting from the heat. I blasted the air-conditioning and talked to her. "We're going to find you a new home," I told her. "And maybe some new teeth."

After driving four hours to Des Moines, I booked a pet-friendly hotel room for one hundred dollars per night—far more than I normally pay with CAPS donor money, but the previous thirty-dollar motel I stayed at had a bed bug infestation. Emma had had enough trauma for one lifetime, so I went out of pocket and we splurged. I opened a can of dog food, watered it down in a coffee mug, and left it in front of Emma's crate. Rescue dogs are typically the victim of too much or too little human contact—Emma fell into the latter category. The Johnsons didn't punch or kick her, but they never walked her or bothered to get her the medical attention she needed. I left her alone until she worked up the courage to investigate her surroundings. Once she was willing to peek outside, I lay on my back and looked away from her. Then I dipped my finger in her food and held it out. I felt a tiny, soft tongue tickling my index finger. I repeated this until the food was gone.

"Good girl, Emma," I said.

I continued to finger-feed Emma until she was ready to lap food from my hand. Always I kept my body low, my gaze away from her. After two days she finally seemed to trust me. Now it was time to get her to a vet.

Emma cowered and squirmed as I picked her up, all the goodwill we had established slipping away. I pressed on, carefully wrapping her in a harness and bringing her outside. She nipped and thrashed as I held her gently but firmly, telling her she'd be okay. I avoided eye contact, which often makes animals more fearful—a trick I learned working undercover at slaughterhouses shackling live chickens and turkeys. I set Emma down, and she immediately went still. She took a few halting steps, sniffed the soft grass, and nibbled on dandelions. The sun was low and the shadows were long as Emma scanned her surroundings like a predator. We were in a grassy field next to a suburban hotel, but to Emma this might as well have been the Serengeti. She glanced at me with wild eyes and then bounded off. I struggled to hold the leash as she dashed into the tall grass. Then she rolled over, shooting her spindly legs into the air and rubbing her butt in the flowers. I realized this was probably Emma's first time playing in the grass. Until then, she had spent her short life living on rocks and rubber mats.

Emma took a few more steps and pooped. Then something caught her eye. She cocked her head and sat down in her own pile of poop. She was staring at the sunset. The colors weren't spectacular, and the sun was descending below a beat-up Silverado in the Ramada parking lot. But I like to think Emma realized, at that moment, she was free to begin her own life. I haven't yet experienced a fall-in-your-own-poop sunset, but I'm sure glad Emma did.

The next day I brought Emma to a vet in Des Moines. He took one look at the medical records Wanda provided for Emma and laughed. Emma's shot record was a handwritten note, with no mention of who gave the shots. The vet ordered all new shots and explained that most of Emma's teeth were so infected they would need to eventually be pulled. But Emma was healthy enough to travel to Boston, where she would live with my girlfriend, whom I'll call Josie, and me until she was ready for a forever home.

(Emma still has half of her teeth—adult dogs have forty-two teeth.

Without all her teeth to chew, she lives every dog's dream of eating only wet food for meals.)

We stayed one night in Indianapolis and then drove sixteen hours to Boston, stopping every three hours for Emma to wander the grass at rest stops. She proved to be an excellent travel buddy, patiently indulging my penchant for heavy metal and punk music. In between Slipknot and Bad Religion tracks, I'd reach back and scratch Emma's paws through the crate. We arrived at my girlfriend's apartment after midnight, and Emma immediately curled up in the hallway and fell asleep.

Training Emma was easier than I expected. At first she needed to be crated at night, but she learned her bathroom schedules within a few days. Like other rescues, Emma responded better to visual rather than verbal cues. I combined exaggerated hand motions with the words *stay* and *come*, which she learned in a matter of hours. After a few days, Emma was scratching at the sofa when Josie and I were watching horror movies, begging for attention. Everything was new to Emma: Cars on the road. Dogs on leashes. People on bicycles. Houses. Sidewalks. Music. Computers. Mirrors. At first she was easily overwhelmed by new sights and sounds and ran for the protection of her crate, which is extremely common with puppy mill dogs. This subsided as Emma learned she had control over where she moved in the house—a freedom puppy mill dogs are denied.

Once she was settled into a routine, I brought Emma to the vet for a more thorough checkup. Twenty of her teeth were so badly rotted they needed to be pulled. An untreated infection in one tooth had managed to bore its way through her skull to the nasal cavity. She also had a heart arrhythmia, which may have been caused by the tooth infection. Unfortunately, none of this is a USDA violation: New guidelines under the Trump administration stipulate that tooth infections are no longer considered veterinary care violations. Even if an inspector did care, there was nothing he or she could do.

Despite losing half her teeth, Emma rebounded amazingly well from surgery. A single toothache would leave me lying in bed all day—but to have twenty rotten teeth, all screaming in pain? It suddenly dawned on me how tough Emma was.

As for Wanda's Li'l Stars, CAPS realized that, despite my footage and reports, the USDA wasn't likely to do a thing. For one, USDA enforcement of the Animal Welfare Act is at a record low. Second, despite the horrendous treatment of Emma, the dying puppy, and her mother with no lower jaw, there were technically few USDA violations present. Dogs are allowed to have rotten teeth. Kennel operators are allowed to treat dying puppies by "hand-feeding"—whatever that means. Thus, the problem is less enforcement of the AWA than the AWA itself. The law is purposefully designed to be vague by an arm of the government established to promote industry—not regulate it. Until we strengthen the AWA or pass entirely new laws, kennels like Wanda's Li'l Stars will continue to operate with impunity.

For now, though, my focus was on Emma. It was time to find her a forever home. Josie and I had fallen in love with her, but with our travel schedules we could not give her the care and attention she deserved. During Emma's final night with us, she curled up on the rug and gazed at me expectantly. I lay down and fell asleep beside her. The next day I brought Emma to Pug Rescue of New England, an excellent home-based rescue group in West Somerville, Massachusetts, that also specializes in Chihuahuas. We met with Tammy Cooper and her husband, Rob, who were flanked by an entourage of rescued Chihuahuas and pugs. Little paws scratched at my feet as Emma bounded off to join in the fun. She became socialized to other dogs much more quickly than I expected. She was eager to sniff and run around the yard with all the other jumping, tail-wagging rescues.

A few days later, Tammy texted me a photo of Emma sleeping beside another Chihuahua, happy and pain-free, and forwarded a video of Emma chasing another dog in the yard, bounding through the grass like a hyper puppy, and finally a photo of Emma wearing a sweater as she sat in front a fireplace, her tiny paws curled up on a dog bed, her big watery eyes above a tiny pink nose.

Emma's permanent home was even better. Tammy and Rob saw Emma get along with their dogs and figured Emma could do well with a companion. They asked their friend Michelle to foster Emma over the Thanksgiving holiday. Michelle's Chihuahua mix, Suzy, bonded with Emma, and the two swiftly became inseparable.

"Pete, I think we found Emma's forever home. I've never seen Emma so happy," Tammy told me.

I had to see for myself, so I visited Tammy's house the day Michelle was scheduled to pick up Emma for good. I was greeted warmly by Tammy, Rob, and their motley crew of misfit rescues. As I stepped into the house, a massive, slobbering yellow Labrador buried her head into me; a French bulldog and pug scampered over with imitation pearl necklaces around their pudgy necks; a blind pug beelined for me, navigating through the entourage of dogs with uncanny precision; and several Chihuahua mixes trotted around me while wagging their tails. Then there was Emma. One ear up, one ear down, the smallest of her ragtag gang. She wore a vest with little pockets on it that made her look like a tiny Han Solo. She walked right up to me with her tail up, letting me pet her cheek. Then Michelle showed up, ready to bring Emma home.

Emma trotted over to Michelle, who began rubbing Emma's cheek. Emma closed her eyes and leaned into Michelle's leg. It was like watching a baby cuddle her mother. Michelle's other dog, Suzy, was bigger than Emma, but friendly and calm. Suzy jumped up on my chair and sat by me, resting her head against my leg. It was almost as if she was saying, "Don't worry, we'll take great care of Emma."

Emma had found her forever home.

PART II

THE RESCUE IN YOUR HOME

WHAT IS A RESCUE DOG?

Now that you know where rescue dogs come from, and what many have been through, let's back up a little and ask a basic question: What is a rescue dog?

The simple answer: A rescue dog is any dog in need of help.

I was surprised the first time I heard someone refer to a dog adopted from a shelter as a "rescue." I'd always thought of a rescue as a dog in need of immediate help from an abusive situation, or one running loose on the street.

But a stray or abused dog needs to be rescued not only *from* the current dire situation but also *into* a loving home so that dog won't be euthanized at a regular shelter, or to free up space for other dogs at a no-kill shelter. This means that everyone who adopts a dog from a shelter is, indeed, a dog rescuer. Adopters don't need catch poles, crates, and blankets to perform a rescue. All they need are compassion, patience, and a loving home.

However, there are important distinctions in how to treat different types of rescue dogs once they are brought home—*if* they should be brought home at all.

To many of us, it seems obvious that we should stop and pick up a stray dog shivering in the rain on the sidewalk. But what if the stray dog is afraid of strangers and acts aggressive?

When I was in the fire academy, I learned about SOPs—standard operating procedures—a common term used in a variety of professions. We learned SOPs for putting on our gear, for holding a fire hose, for providing emergency medical services, and so on. In every class that I took at the academy, someone would always ask about exceptions to SOPs. "Should you really wait for backup if you hear someone screaming just past the doorway? What if backup is too far away, by the truck?" Veteran firefighters usually responded, "There's book world, and there's real world."

Book-world SOPs were designed to help us pass tests, get certified, and train for situations so hectic that we needed to develop habits to override fear and instinct. However, I saw the best firefighters throw the rule book away whenever they needed to.

As an investigator, I've created SOP lists for working cases and training investigators. I've also broken every SOP I've ever created, because the real world doesn't always conform to the book world. A quick example: Most dog trainers will tell you to put your new dog into a crate to house-train the animal. But is it really a good idea to place a dog just adopted from a puppy mill, who has spent her entire life living in a cage, into a crate in your home? Probably not.

The following are some SOPs to help you care for dogs rescued from the street, from abusive situations, from disaster areas, from loving foster homes, and from shelters. Be prepared to break every rule I give you whenever necessary.

Wags, Hope, and Healing and Phoenix

In July 2016, an adoring two-year-old gray pit bull sat outside a bar in the small town of Victoria, Texas. Tied to the bumper of a truck, the dog waited for his guardian to finish drinking at a bar before they could drive home. But the man in the bar came back to the truck drunk, forgot he'd tied his dog to the truck, and drove off.

The dog was dragged for a mile down the road before his guardian finally realized that the honking vehicles nearby were telling him to pull over. The pit bull had tried to keep up with the speeding truck, but it was impossible. Gravel had torn into his skin and to the bones of his front left leg and both rear legs. He lost a toe, and two toes on his back right paw were broken. Bleeding,

too injured to stand, the dog, along with his drunk owner, waited on a country road until animal control arrived to rescue the dog and have the guardian arrested.

Because the dog was evidence in a cruelty case against his guardian, he was held for five days by animal control where, in constant pain, he needed pain meds and extensive physical therapy. He also needed help to recover mentally to find a new home. That is where the dog's luck turned around.

Jennifer Carroll runs Wags, Hope and Healing, an animal rescue in Johnson City, Texas. Wags specializes in taking animals from cruelty, neglect, and hoarding cases all over the state. The organization has close ties with law enforcement, which can call on Wags for their expertise in animal rescue and rehabilitation. When Wags heard about the severely injured pit bull, they immediately took the dog. They named him, with hope in their hearts, Phoenix.

Phoenix was on pain meds for two weeks and able to do very little for himself. Whenever workers and volunteers went to sit with Phoenix to feed and care for him, all he wanted to do was kiss their faces and melt in their laps. He had a slow road to recovery; he needed to be placed in a large bathtub once a day so water pressure could stimulate oxygen into his wounds to promote healing. To recover muscles that were literally torn away, Phoenix took short walks on a leash, limping along as caretakers patiently praised him for his gradual progress. When therapy was done, he would crawl into people's laps and rest his huge head on their chests. He was so gentle and loving that he developed a fan club, and people regularly came to bring him presents.

After three months he was physically healed, but Phoenix was not entirely in the clear. He was still a giant pit bull. Despite being a dog with soulful watery eyes who simply wanted to cuddle all day, most people thought Phoenix was in the shelter because he had done something bad. But like the other pit bulls Wags has rescued and adopted out, Phoenix was no danger to anyone.

After a worrisome couple of months, Phoenix's rescue was complete. A therapist who treated soldiers for post-traumatic stress disorder saw Phoenix for who he truly was and understood his physical scars didn't mean his mental scars couldn't be overcome. When they first met, Phoenix crawled right into the woman's arms. Phoenix soon became best friends with the therapist's other dog, a boxer, and within a year had learned to be a therapy dog to help soldiers with PTSD.

Understanding a Rescue Dog

Before we get into specifics, it's important to understand not only dogs' behavior but also our relationship with dogs.

Dogs have lived with people as our companions and been integral parts of human cultures for millennia—perhaps 32,000 years. Having evolved socially alongside dogs, we may find it natural to treat them as surrogate children, and for dogs to treat us as surrogate parents. However, the introduction of dogs into human culture most likely had a more practical origin, when wolflike animals alerted our ancestors to possible danger in exchange for feeding off the leftovers of animals we hunted for food. This mutually beneficial relationship allowed these wild creatures to evolve into what we now know as dogs while leaving their lupine instincts intact. (The current scientific thinking is that dogs did not descend directly from wolves but share a wolflike ancestor with them.)

Lupine instincts are only one of the factors that shape the behavior of wolves and dogs. As with people and many other animals, much of their behavior is learned. Normally, both wolves and dogs learn to cooperate in family units and do not try to lord it over one another in an instinctive struggle for dominance.

This fact contradicts the common belief that dogs need an "alpha" member who dominates the others in the pack. Many dog trainers believe that a dog's guardian must play the alpha role and render their dog submissive. I strongly disagree. I believe dogs see themselves as our equals, a point that probably runs counter to everything you've learned about them.

To appreciate this point, it's necessary to understand two very different situations: how dogs treat one another when they are forced to form a pack for survival and how they treat one another within their natural family packs.

The concept that dogs have a hierarchy comes from rather unscientific observations of wolves living at Zoo Basel in Basel, Switzerland, during the 1930s and 1940s. The wolves there were taken from two different packs and held in captivity. To work together as a single pack at the zoo, the animals had to construct a social system that developed over the course of their lives rather than the course of their species' evolution. Further studies of wolves captured from their original environments and placed into areas where they were forced to live together have reinforced the concept that all wolf packs have an alpha male and an established social order.

In the wild, however, wolf packs consist of a mother, a father, and cubs who then mature and go off to start families of their own.

In other words: It is not in a dog's nature to have a dominant alpha lording it over her while she acts submissive. Instead, her instinct is to be part of a family. Certainly, there are times when one family member will dominate another. You can't very well let the dog pee on the carpet or bite the mail carrier. And there are some things the dog simply can't let you do, like eat all the popcorn on movie night. Clearly, only a few pieces belong to the dog.

I believe the reason many people want to dominate their dogs comes from a misunderstanding of both dog evolution and canine behavior. The reasons we race dogs, fight dogs, show dogs for their physical characteristics, and breed dogs for medical experimentation say a lot about us but very little about dogs. These reasons also greatly affect how we treat them. But to understand dog behavior correctly, we have to see dogs for exactly who they are and not who we want them to be. Too often, we view animals through a lens blurred by the belief that other creatures exist for our purposes rather than for their own.

Just as we have bred cattle, hogs, and chickens for our own purposes, so, too, have we bred dogs for our own reasons. The many roles dogs have played for us in the past—such as helping us hunt or raising our social status—were created not by nature but by people. Even if we believe those purposes were justified, that is no reason to continue exploiting dogs now.

It is true that dogs' instincts are shaped by their breeding, and that dogs will feel more fulfilled when following their instincts. Many terrier breeds, for example, want to explore tight spaces such as under beds or beneath fallen logs. But how our ancestors shaped these dogs' appearance and behavior should play no role in how we view them today. We need to appreciate them as beings that exist for their own reasons and are not only capable of happiness, love, loyalty, and respect, but also worthy of those things themselves.

Any past benefits we may have gained from breeding dogs have been overshadowed by the harms of overbreeding: stray dogs and overcrowded shelters. Moreover, breeding dogs solely for their physical appearance has created animals almost guaranteed to suffer from breed-specific health problems. Pugs have eye issues, boxers develop hip dysplasia, and English bulldogs face a list of health issues including respiratory and joint problems. Breeding dogs for medical experimentation assumes we have the right to make dogs suffer for us, which stems from the belief that the purpose of dogs is to serve us—even if it means sacrificing their lives.

So if you want to have a happy dog in your home, remember that your dog doesn't want to be dominated. Your dog doesn't want to fear you. Your dog doesn't want to please you at the expense of her own health or happiness. Your dog wants a friend. Your dog can learn her own purpose when she's a happy part of your family, and you can learn from the purpose and fulfillment you gain in loving and being loved by your rescued dog.

Julie and Violet

Julie Germany lives just outside of Washington, DC, in northern Virginia. Once a political grassroots and digital consultant, Julie ran a think tank at George Washington University focusing on technology and democracy, and then ran an organization designed to interest millennials in the processes of democracy. When the time was right, Julie joined forces with a friend to run the White Coat Waste Project, originated to end taxpayer-funded experiments on dogs, cats, monkeys, and other animals—the government currently spends as much as $15 billion on animal experiments. One victory from 2017 to 2018 helped defund dog experiments at the US Department of Veterans Affairs.

This line of work helped Julie meet Violet. Julie was doing volunteer work at a downtown DC animal laboratory. The lab allowed volunteers to come in, take animals out of the cages, and play with them. Violet was the first dog Julie met. A fifty-pound hound, Violet was about a year old, with copper coloring and very big, very sad eyes.

Although she was terrified of people, Violet did allow Julie to play with her when other dogs were around. She didn't really know how to interact with humans; her only contact with them was as a guinea pig. But she was sweet and very fearful, and Julie knew when she returned Violet to her cage that she had to save her from this life. The laboratory allowed people to adopt dogs when they had finished two studies. After that, if the dogs weren't adopted, they were enrolled in terminal studies in which, for example, they were killed and their organs harvested and studied.

Violet's two studies were difficult—in one, she was tested at a medical school, where she was a test dummy for operations. Then she was used in a human pharmaceutical test. But she persevered, and finally she was available for a real home. Julie swept in and adopted her.

It wasn't an easy transition. Violet was terrified of many things. Julie and her husband tried to get the dog to play outside, but she was scared—she had never seen anything outside of a laboratory before. The wind, the rain, the noise all frightened her. She was also frightened of the house, and it took her months to get up the nerve to explore it—and even then, if spooked, she would dash back to her safe spot, a dog playpen Julie set up filled with blankets and pillows in the den. Violet's life was made easier, however, by Julie's rescue cats, who instantly fell for Violet and spent hours kneading and comforting her. Violet also seldom made any sounds. Julie assumed she had been debarked, a common occurrence at labs when the staff decides they just can't stand all the barking and cut the dogs' vocal cords. But after a few months, Violet suddenly barked. From then on, she became vocally expressive.

Today, Violet still has issues: She suffers from tremendous separation anxiety and pitches a fit whenever Julie or her husband leaves the house. But for the most part she has settled into her routine, helping Julie and her husband with all the other animals they're taking care of. Violet might not trust humans, for good reason, but she feels safe with other animals and loves to be around them and cuddle with them.

A year and a half after Violet was rescued, her family adopted a ginger kitten named Trucker Cat, who was abandoned on a highway in rural Virginia. Violet helped Trucker Cat adjust to life in his new home, and they became fast buddies, sleeping together, begging for snacks together. Since then, Julie and her husband have fostered more than twenty rescue kittens from the island of St. Croix, and Violet has helped each batch of kittens adjust to life in their foster home.

Why Rescue?

To Save a Life

By adopting a rescue, you are saving a life. If you have the time, energy, and finances to include a dog in your family, adopting can be an extraordinary, life-changing event for both the dog and you. (If you can't adopt, fostering dogs or volunteering at shelters also save dogs' lives.)

Rescue dogs take patience, care, understanding, and love—but so do all dogs. It's a misconception that rescue dogs are somehow broken and will take more work than purpose-bred dogs. In fact, considering breeders' practices of removing puppies from their mothers too early and of breeding dogs solely for their physical appearance, behavioral and health issues occur far more commonly in the latter.

To Find a Healthier Dog

Adopting a rescue dog can help ensure that you are getting a healthier dog than one you might buy at a pet store. The deplorable conditions at puppy mills, like the ones you've read about, coupled with the punishing routines of breeding dogs chosen for physical characteristics that meet a breed standard but not a health standard, can lead to numerous physical problems. The animals in puppy mills are stuffed into small cages in confined areas, leading to the quick spread of illnesses in puppies too young for vaccines to take effect. Other illnesses can spread regardless of whether puppies have been vaccinated or dewormed because these crowded, stress-inducing conditions often suppress their immune systems. (This is why puppies with impressive health records and a fantastic health guarantee from a pet store can quickly show signs of respiratory infections after you take them home.)

If you adopt a grown dog from a shelter, you also won't have to worry about one of the worst illnesses dogs can get: canine parvovirus, which often damages puppies' intestines, affecting their ability to absorb nutrients and eventually leading to death. Parvo mostly affects puppies because dogs tend to have better-developed immune systems.

Puppy mills are also less likely than shelters to invest resources into saving puppies. As we learned in Part 1 of this book, instead of viewing puppies as individual lives to be saved, as shelters do, mill owners view puppies as livestock. With commercial breeders, the bottom line is not how many lives are saved; the bottom line is money. The breeder must decide if it's worth the time and effort to isolate and treat a dying puppy in the same way a hog farmer decides whether a sow with a broken leg should be treated, killed, or sent off to slaughter for a few more dollars. Cost-effectiveness does not mean better veterinary care but doing just enough to get puppies out the door and off to the store, after which any health problems that come up are someone else's problem.

Also consider that store dogs are seldom, if ever, checked by a veterinarian.

The puppies at the pet store may look cute and healthy, but things are not always what they seem. During my time working undercover at Hunte and at a Petland, one of a chain of US stores supplied by puppy mills, I saw firsthand how illnesses not only were able to travel quickly from puppy to puppy in the cramped conditions of brokerage facilities, trucks, and stores, but that many illnesses didn't become apparent until the puppies were already on the truck or at the store.

A CVI, also known as a health certificate, is an official document issued by an accredited agency. It certifies that the animals on the document have been inspected and are healthy enough to be transported from one place to another. CAPS, the nonprofit for which I've investigated hundreds of puppy mills and pet stores, obtains CVIs to determine where puppies at pet stores come from. However, I've found that CVIs don't mean much when it comes to puppies purchased from breeders. As you read, at Hunte, the largest broker of puppy mill dogs in the country, I watched vets give a two-second glance to puppies and then write them up as perfectly healthy. I also saw that puppies with paperwork stamped HEALTHY by those vets had been examined not by licensed professionals but by unqualified kennel staff. Martin Creek Kennels managed to beat the system by having their vet sign CVIs for several or even dozens of dogs at a time without even seeing a single dog.

This practice does not happen at shelters. Shelters don't try to send dogs out across state lines and then ignore your phone call if the dog gets sick. They are far more concerned with the health of the rescue than the price you paid to adopt one, and they will go to greater lengths to ensure their dogs are healthy before being put up for adoption.

To Avoid Dogs with Behavioral Issues

Concern over behavioral issues is a major reason people adopt puppies from breeders instead of shelters. It's a common worry that shelter dogs, who were once lost, abused, or given up by their caregivers, may have behavioral problems due to their pasts. People also assume that puppies from breeders, who are raised from birth, are more likely to have desirable personalities.

Actually, it's the other way around. Most puppy mills remove puppies from their mothers at about six weeks of age or sooner. The puppies can't legally be sold until about eight weeks of age, but it's common practice to get them out of the whelping box and into cages to make room for the next litter. That way, they can speed the mama dog's recovery so she can start breeding again. Removing puppies too early from their mothers like this leads to separation anxiety, fear of other dogs, and biting (because the puppies never learned from their mother and siblings how to play without being too rough).

To Find a Dog with the Right Personality

Rescue dogs' personalities are readily apparent, unlike those of puppies from a mill or store. At a shelter, dogs' individual traits are better known to the kennel staff and volunteers. Sometimes the animals will already have begun training, so kennel workers will be able to tell you if certain dogs like other dogs, cats, or kids; how they do on a leash; and other facets of their personalities.

Mick McAuliffe has extensive experience in this arena. He's the director of animal services at Animal Rescue League of Iowa (ARL) in Des Moines, a facility that has taken in dogs rescued during my investigations in Iowa. According to Mick, no one can say for certain that a dog's behavior at a shelter will mimic how that dog will act in a home environment. That said, Mick—who has worked as an explosive-detection dog handler/trainer for the Australian Army and the US Department of Defense and handled bomb-sniffing dogs in Afghanistan—swears by using rescues for these life-and-death jobs. As he put it, "You know what you're getting."

Of course, some otherwise wonderful shelter dogs do have behavioral issues. But shelters including ARL usually know how to handle them and can give ongoing advice after you've adopted your dog. A good shelter will be completely open with you about a dog's behavior in general and will prepare you for any problems that shelter staff have had to deal with. As Mick says, "Honesty from shelters is very important. ARL wants to give adopters all the info they can to help them make the most informed decision they can."

That's not the case with a breeder. Buy a few-weeks-old puppy from a breeder and you don't really know what you are getting. That puppy, regardless of her behavior at the moment, could turn out to be sociable, fearful, playful, or aggressive with other dogs. And, based on her early upbringing, a dog from a breeder is less likely to be well adjusted.

There's nothing in the Animal Welfare Act (the regulations that USDA-licensed puppy mills are supposed to follow) that requires puppy mills to consider the emotional well-being of their dogs. And unfortunately, it's apparent from how the mills confine and breed them for a profit that they don't. Shelters, however, consider the psychological well-being of dogs a top priority and will make their best effort to rehabilitate problem dogs. All animals are different, but if you adopt a dog from a shelter, there is a much higher chance that you will know who that dog actually is ahead of time.

For example, my girlfriend, Josie, has a purebred Jack Russell terrier named Floyd. Josie got Floyd from a breeder when she was nineteen and working at a vet's office. (This was before she met me, obviously!) A sweet, tiny, ten-week-old puppy, Floyd was so small he fit inside a coat pocket.

Once Josie brought him home, tiny Floyd's true nature emerged. Despite constant effort, nobody in Josie's family was able to control Floyd's excitable personality or calm him down when needed. When Floyd was younger, he had one setting when he was outdoors: full berserk. He would charge through the woods all day and not return until nightfall. If he got off leash, no amount of yelling or coaxing would get him to come back. At age twelve, Floyd developed glaucoma, which eventually caused him to go blind and to suffer constant eye pain that required both of his eyes to be removed. Floyd then switched to a different setting: blind berserk. With his stubby little tail twitching behind his stout body, front paws pattering in short steps as he feels out where he's going, Floyd now sets off in one direction and doesn't stop. When he bumps into something, he changes direction and keeps going. He is the Roomba of the forest.

Nobody could have predicted Floyd would be so adventurous, so relentless in his desire to explore, even while blind. Fortunately for him, Josie is a dog lover who has run marathons and has the energy to keep up. But for many people, this cute puppy from a breeder would have been far too much to handle.

Eric and Peety

In 2010, Eric O'Grey, who currently works for Physicians Committee for Responsible Medicine, was 340 pounds and taking fifteen different medications for a variety of conditions, including type 2 diabetes. He was on three different antidepressants, blood pressure medication, statins, and medications intended to alleviate the side effects of other medications. Eric had been morbidly obese for twenty-five years. The hundreds of visits to doctors didn't help. All he ever got were prescriptions and the recommendation that he diet and exercise. No one ever explained exactly what that meant. His last doctor looked at his stats and told him he needed to purchase a cemetery plot soon.

Shortly after that, Eric was traveling on an airplane. Because the crew had run out of seat belt extensions, they couldn't buckle Eric into his seat properly, delaying the flight for forty-five minutes. The other passengers called him names and swore at him. This was, he thought, the nadir of his life.

When he returned from his trip, Eric happened to turn on the television and caught an interview with former president Bill Clinton talking about his health, and how a whole-food, plant-based diet had turned it around. Eric was impressed. He had already tried thirty-six different diets and none of them worked. However, his current doctor did not really understand what a whole-food, plant-based diet was, so Eric found a new doctor who recommended a new course of treatment. She was already on such a diet, and she recommended not only that he do the same but also that he adopt a dog. Eric had never had a dog. Nor, at that point, had he any friends, and he barely ever went outside. The doctor said he needed exercise, which walking a dog would give him, and it might help his social life as well.

Eric got in touch with the Humane Society Silicon Valley and, after thinking it over, instead of asking for a cute puppy, requested an obese middle-aged dog so the two would have much in common. After a series of interviews the shelter brought him Peety, a dog who was hugely overweight, covered with rashes, missing patches of fur, and walking with his head hung low to the ground. No one wanted this dog. Eric felt the same way about himself—no one wanted him, either. When the human and the canine finally made eye contact, Eric sensed that they both felt disappointment. But the people at the shelter said, "This is your dog. He needs you as much as you need him. You will both be better off with each other."

So Eric took the dog. At first it was difficult for both of them, but slowly they both began to diet and exercise. It worked. Peety grew to love Eric. "He had such confidence in me I developed confidence in myself, never felt unconditional love before. I started to become a different person, the person Peety thought I was." And Eric fell for his problematic, overweight dog just as much.

Eric consulted with a veterinarian, who worked out a plant-based diet for Peety that consisted primarily of tofu, quinoa, and legumes. Soon Peety lost twenty-five pounds, his skin improved, his rashes disappeared. Likewise, in five months Eric was off all his medications, had reversed his type 2 diabetes, and within a year had lost 140 pounds. His cholesterol dropped from 400 to 120. His waist size went from 52 to 33.

The two lived a happy and fulfilling life together until Peety's death in 2015. Eric then wrote a book about his life with his dog called *Walking with Peety: The Dog Who Saved My Life*.

CHOOSING A RESCUE

I s adopting a dog right for you?

If you ever find yourself thinking, *I suddenly feel like I want a dog, and I want one right now*, then please: Slow down, eat a whole chocolate cake, and get the need to indulge yourself out of your system. Do not impulse-buy a dog!

First, you need to make sure you have the time, energy, and finances to care for a dog for his or her entire life. Generally, it costs about $1,000 to take care of a dog during the first year of life and about $500 a year after that. This budget does not include emergency veterinary care or pet health insurance. If you add training, day care, or dog walkers, the cost will rise considerably. So if you can't afford it, don't do it.

Your schedule will need to be adjusted as well. As you'll read in the section on training, you'll want to make sure you have time to help your dog learn, or refresh, basic house-training skills. But most important, you will need to exercise your dog often. A dog has to be able to burn off energy and feel stimulated. This can't be overstated: Exercise is critical for bonding with your dog, reducing unwanted behavior, and ensuring that training will be successful. If you don't have the time, don't get a dog.

I myself don't have the time. I travel too much. I do, however, foster dogs from puppy mills and volunteer at shelters. Fostering a dog means keeping him temporarily until a permanent home is found or a shelter has space to take him. Volunteering is exactly what you think—and you'll read more about how to do it in Part 3.

If you're ready to adopt a dog, or just thinking about where to find one, there are more options than you might realize. Shelters are the most common choice, but another good option is tapping foster home networks.

These networks, also commonly called rescue groups, are composed of individuals who take in stray and abandoned dogs as well as shelter dogs who are about to be euthanized. The difference between a shelter and a foster network is that foster networks don't have staff or dedicated facilities. They're just regular people who pool resources to save as many dogs as they can. Rescue networks often use social media pages to communicate with one another and with the public. Sometimes groups adopt out dogs at pet supply stores, such as Petco and PetSmart, and individual members may also meet with potential adopters individually.

Breed-specific rescues and foster home networks, which exist all over the country, are a vital tool in the dog-rescue movement. They take in dogs of only a certain breed, often searching local shelters to rescue dogs of the breed they care for. With so many people buying puppies from breeders, breed-specific rescue groups offer you the option of being able to adopt the type of dog you want, saving a life, and not having to support a puppy mill.

Friends for Life and Emma

Houston-based Friends For Life is one of Texas's premier no-kill shelters, and often works with animals whom other shelters typically turn down, no matter how badly off the dog might be.

A typical example of Friends For Life's work is Emma. Found wandering in the woods just prior to Hurricane Harvey, Emma was in terrible condition, barely alive, and petrified. The kind woman who discovered Emma brought her into her home, fearing the dog would not survive the storm. Yet after Harvey had passed, the woman was not allowed back into her house, which she'd had to evacuate without her animals; she had moved them to the second floor, hoping desperately they could escape the flooding. Amazingly, they all survived.

According to the shelter, "The day we met Emma, the sight of her malnourished body and her terrified spirit broke our hearts. Emma's skin was so ravaged by severe infection that it hung from her frame in bloody pouches. Her long, never-trimmed nails curled under in grotesque claws, and even after Emma's nails had been cut to a healthy length, she still struggled to walk under the weight of the trauma."

The Friends For Life team gently bathed Emma, who was terrified of being touched. But she needed countless baths to address the out-of-control infection that had been destroying her skin for such a long time. She was in far worse condition than the staff originally thought: so much of her fur was gone they couldn't even tell what color she was, and she was covered with wounds from incessantly scratching herself.

It turned out that Emma was suffering from a highly unusual bacterial infection resistant to most medicines. The staff had to wear gloves to apply her medications because they couldn't touch them—just a bit of contact could damage a human's liver. These medications had to be administered every eight hours, so a devoted staff member had to attend to Emma all day and all night to combat the infection.

Finally, as she improved, Emma was taken to a medical foster home, where she continued to heal from not only the physical infections but also from the emotional scars of so many years of neglect. But Emma was a survivor, and after just ten days with her medical foster moms, her hair and skin had improved tremendously. Even better, Emma's spirit was healing as well.

Emma stayed at Friends For Life for about seven months, constantly learning how to lose her fear of humans. Luckily, Emma did trust and like other dogs, so she was roomed with a fellow canine whom she quickly bonded with. Emma's mood improved so dramatically that she was put up for adoption and was swiftly taken by a woman who was dealing with the recent death of a pet. Her surviving dog had become so lonely he seemed unable to cope with daily life. But when these two dogs met, it was love at first sight. Emma still had issues, but according to her new family, they slowly melted away in her new home.

Rescues and False Rescues

Rescue groups can be excellent sources from which to adopt a dog. There are a few concerns, however. Rescue groups are not always registered as nonprofits, nor are their members' homes inspected, so you must do a little homework first. And you must be on the lookout for groups known as false rescues.

False rescue groups try to pass off puppies bought from commercial dog breeders as actual rescues. These groups vary: Some are independent organizations that realize they can turn a profit buying puppies from breeders and selling them to the unsuspecting public; others are created by puppy mills as another market for their dogs. Most commonly, false rescue puppies are sold in pet stores that are not legally allowed to sell puppies from breeders but are permitted to sell ones from rescue groups. At other times, false rescues sell these puppies at adoption events in public places or at pet supply stores just as local no-kill shelters do.

Fortunately, it's easier than you might think to spot a false rescue group and to find a good real one. Here's a list of what to look for to make sure a rescue group is legitimate.

Does the group adopt out mixed-breed dogs or exclusively purebred puppies?

The biggest giveaway of a false rescue groups is selling purebred puppies they claim were rescued from puppy mills. Rescuing puppies from puppy mills rarely happens. Rescuing the adult breeding dogs is more common. If the group has only purebred puppies, it's practically a dead giveaway they are a false rescue. Remember, too, that while breed-specific rescues will offer rescued purebred dogs, they won't have only puppies of a single breed.

How much are they charging?

Most shelters charge no more than $200 to adopt a dog, while quite a few charge considerably less. If the price is many hundreds of dollars, especially for purebred puppies, you are probably dealing with a false rescue group.

Do they work with a shelter?

Many dogs cared for by foster home networks are strays, but if the rescue group gets dogs from a shelter to prevent them from being euthanized, that shelter will have heard of the rescue group. A good rescue group should be able to tell you where they get the dogs, and you should follow up on that information.

Does the group have a public identity?

False rescue groups generally have little to no public profile, as the people associated with them don't want their names or photos appearing on social media. Legitimate rescue workers tend to make their identity very public, as they want publicity for their dogs. Their profile usually consists of a website with information about the people running the group, especially if they are a registered nonprofit, and/or social media accounts with frequent updates. For example, you can tell that Suruluna, a superb rescue outfit in upstate New York, is legit just by looking at its passionate, persistent social media presence highlighting its dogs and the dogs' stories.

Shelters, on the other hand, are physical facilities that keep dogs and allow the public to visit for adoptions. A wide variety of shelters exist: Some are nonprofits and survive solely through donations, while others are municipal facilities run by a local government and funded through a tax subsidy. If shelters have a euthanasia rate of 10 percent or lower, they are called no-kill shelters.

No-kill shelters are generally wonderful and important facilities—but how they operate depends on their circumstances. Some no-kill shelters turn away dogs to avoid becoming overpopulated, while others overpopulate, creating poor living conditions. Some have fewer adoptions because they don't have sufficient funds to pay for outreach programs. Some with low dog intakes will go out of their way to save dogs from high-euthanasia facilities. Some shelters have a large crew of dedicated volunteers and donors, allowing them to work with foster home networks and adopt out dogs at pet supply stores in addition to directly from their shelter.

One example of an excellent no-kill shelter is Austin Pets Alive!

(APA) in Austin, Texas. APA works with Austin Animal Center (AAC), Austin's city animal control facility. AAC did not start out with a no-kill mission. But with the help of Austin Pets Alive!, the city government, realizing that the public supported the concept, created an auxiliary no-kill city shelter. Under the agreement, APA takes the least-adoptable dogs—those who have behavioral or health issues—from AAC so that the city won't have to euthanize them. The arrangement has given AAC a euthanasia rate so low (0.5 percent) that AAC can claim to be the largest no-kill municipal shelter in the country, and Austin the largest no-kill city in the US, for many years now. APA has achieved a 98 percent live release rate, meaning that 98 percent of the dogs who enter the no-kill shelter are adopted to families. Two-thirds of APA's rescue dogs live in foster homes, and the rest are at the shelter, continuing the training and socialization the shelter specializes in.

Adopting a dog from Austin Pets Alive! is a great idea, but so is adopting from Austin Animal Center.

All that said, I strongly feel a shelter's no-kill status shouldn't be the determining factor in adopting from that facility or not. There's a need for dogs to be rescued from both types of shelters. Either a dog needs to be adopted from a no-kill shelter so more space can be freed up to rescue another dog, or a dog needs to be rescued from another shelter so that the animal isn't euthanized. Both ways, a life is saved.

There are a variety of other factors that can determine if a particular shelter is right for you. First and foremost, if the shelter you're at has the dog you want, then you've found the right place. Despite anything else you read in this book—or any other—when you see a particular shelter dog who looks into your eyes with hope or joy, lies curled up in a corner with loneliness, or wags her tail with enthusiasm, you'll just *know* that you've found the right dog. Sometimes, dogs pick us.

The following are some things to consider when determining whether a shelter is a reliable place from which to adopt dogs.

Mark and Georgia

In 2004, Mark Graham, a kitchen designer liv-
ing outside of Philadelphia, adopted a shelter
dog named Bubba. Bubba lived with Mark and
his husband, Bob, for thirteen years. When
Bubba died, Mark considered adopting a new
dog but wanted some time to grieve.

However, not long after Bubba passed, a
friend sent the couple a note about a ten-year-
old Jack Russell mix who was up for adoption. Mark didn't have
much interest in the dog, but because Bob did, they went to look
at her. It didn't go well: "The dog had no interest in us. All she
wanted to do was pee and leave," Mark explained.

Seeing that dog, however, made them realize that a rescue dog
was in their near future, so they checked out another shelter. "I'm
a firm believer that when it's the right dog, you just know it in
your heart," Mark says. "We turned a corner and came face-to-face
with a cute brown dog with the most gorgeous butterscotch-
colored eyes. And I knew right then that this was the dog."

A fifty-pound Lab mix, she was, Mark says, the happiest, most
alert dog they had seen in the place. She was also wearing the
dreaded cone of shame with a sign above her kennel that read NOT
AVAILABLE FOR ADOPTION. Mark stopped one of the workers and
asked for an explanation. He said that the dog had had surgery
earlier in the week and was still healing. Once she was better, she
would be available to meet and be adopted. By this point Mark was
crouched down, petting her though the bars, giving her little
treats.

"What surgery did she have?" he asked. Bob looked at him
oddly. "Have you even looked at the dog?"

Mark took a closer look and realized she was missing her right hind leg. Apparently the dog, who had come to the shelter from the South a few weeks previously, had, somewhere along her long life as a stray, broken her right hind leg very badly. It was unworkable, so the shelter decided the only option was to amputate it.

This didn't bother Mark at all—mostly because it didn't bother the soon-to-be-named Georgia (so named to honor her Southern background). In fact, the couple found her to be the most energetic and radiant dog they saw all day, despite her cone and her missing leg. Moreover, she was missing a toe on her remaining hind paw, was heartworm positive, and had an ear infection, conjunctivitis, gingivitis, and tartar on her teeth. They still wanted her. And, Mark says, she wanted them. The bond was quick and strong.

They ended up waiting a week and then were able to take her home, cone and all. The stitches came out a week later, but one night Mark noticed that the wound was oozing pus. They took her to an emergency animal hospital and discovered that the surgeon had left two stitches in her incision and Georgia had developed a bad infection. The vet prescribed such a heavy-duty antibiotic that Mark was instructed to use latex gloves rather than touch the pills with his bare skin.

After three weeks, Georgia pulled through. She is, Mark says, a truly happy dog who doesn't let the lack of a hind leg bother her. "Every sofa in the house is fair game for her, as are all the beds—she even has no problem getting in and out of the car by herself." All they have to do is make sure she doesn't become overweight, as that would put too much pressure on the joints in the other legs.

Today Georgia is about five, and as Mark says, she's very popular in the neighborhood because "when you walk a three-legged dog, people notice. And she has these ASPCA advertisement eyes, the ones that make you fall in love with her immediately. The other day she saw a man coming down the street who had been buying ice cream; she stopped and stared right at him until the man finally offered to give her some. This is her superpower. She can get anyone to give her food."

Does the shelter provide the dogs with regular exercise?

Important in helping the dogs' mental as well as their physical well-being, exercise can transform their stay from frightening and uncomfortable to enjoyable. Also, regular trips out of their kennels help abandoned dogs who are house-trained remain house-trained rather than reverting to soiling their new sleeping area.

Does the shelter offer the dogs regular human contact?

A shelter that simply puts dogs into a pen, feeds them twice a day, cleans out their runs once a day, and then euthanizes them when time runs out is not a good operation. Adoption rates increase and return rates of dogs brought back by adopters decrease when dogs are socialized and comforted by shelter staff and volunteers.

Does the shelter train the dogs?

If dogs are taught basic commands such as "sit" and "stay" and not to bite, they gain valuable lessons that benefit their adopters and receive much-needed mental stimulation as well. The Animal Rescue League of Iowa has an extensive training program focused on positive reinforcement and creating positive associations with people. The shelter doesn't use physical or verbal corrections and refuses to use choke collars or shock collars. They focus first on helping dogs to become calm in their new environment. Once this is achieved, the dogs can learn simple training commands quickly.

Australian-born Mick McAuliffe of ARL points out that shock collars are illegal in southern Australia. Simply putting one on your dog could get you a $10,000 fine or a year in jail. Mick, whose life depended on training and teaming up with bomb-sniffing dogs in the field, is confused as to why people think shock collars are needed in the United States when they aren't in Australia. It makes no sense, he says: Dogs are dogs everywhere.

Does the shelter offer information about where the dogs came from and/or their personalities?

When dogs are brought to a good shelter by their owners, the staff gathers all the information they can about them, including: Are the dogs house-trained? Do they like other dogs or cats? Are they used to being around children? And so on. Many shelters obtain this information by having dedicated volunteers foster dogs before the dogs spend time at the shelter.

Stray dogs may have unknown histories, but the kennel staff can learn these dogs' personalities if they spend time with them. They can determine if a particular dog gets along with other dogs by introducing them to other animals on leashes, first in controlled environments and then in playgroups. They can discover whether the dog likes cats by walking him past felines to see if the dog reacts calmly or fixates on them, possibly indicating aggression.

Ideally, this information will be posted publicly and is commonly listed on cards on the dogs' enclosures.

Does the shelter want to adopt out a dog to you immediately, or do they take the time to pair you with the right animal?

Good shelters will ask you many questions about your lifestyle and experience with dogs. They can also help you understand that a dog's personality counts for more than that dog's physical characteristics— meaning you may end up with a rescue who is a different shape and size than you had anticipated. Good shelters will help match you with the dog most likely to be a lifelong companion rather than just trying to get another dog out the door.

Does the shelter recommend tips for training your rescue, keeping your rescue secure in your yard, or just living with a dog if you've never had one before?

Good shelters have training information on hand and will be available to help you out with advice for as long as your rescue is alive. Advice on training and keeping your home safe for your dog are an important part of a successful adoption.

Dispelling Shelter Myth

Shelter Dogs Are Crazy

Shelter dogs come from a variety of backgrounds. Yes, some have been abused, but the majority are given up by their owners. While dogs at shelters might have separation anxiety after being dumped by their previous families, they have had the advantage of being looked after by shelter staff and volunteers. Also, depending on the shelter, it is quite likely they have been given training and attention, and have been walked, groomed, and played with. They are certainly given more space than a tiny pet store cage that allows them little more than a space in which to pace back and forth.

Shelter Dogs Have Bad Habits

My experience at no-kill shelters has shown me that most rescues once lived in a home. They are often house-trained, know not to bite people's hands when playing, and understand the concept of riding in a car and how to walk on a leash. Rescues are far more likely than pet store puppies to have good habits.

Shelter Dogs Can't Be Trained

As explained earlier, shelter dogs are often already trained. Many shelters have staff and volunteers who work to find out if any behavioral issues exist and then take steps to handle them. No-kill shelters specifically have volunteers or foster "parents" teach dogs basic commands such as "sit," "stay," and "come." These shelters are likely to give you information about what your new rescue has learned in training and which training methods were used. This way, you can follow up with the same methods and be assured your dog is not only capable of being trained but also used to it.

Rescuing Dogs off the Street

What's the most common form of dog rescue that doesn't involve adopting a dog from a shelter? Finding and adopting a stray dog off the street.

Unfortunately, many misconceptions surround this kind of rescue, which is very much site specific: Rescuing a stray dog in the suburbs is entirely different from rescuing a stray dog in the city, which in turn differs from rescuing a stray dog in a rural area. I've driven with activists through the countryside on dirt roads with nothing around us but farms. When we see fat dogs trotting along these roads or plodding through the fields, the activists often ask if we should stop to help. They're accustomed from their city experience to assume that a loose dog is a stray dog. That's not always the case in the country. Dogs in rural areas often run loose, having an entire farm, and perhaps far beyond, as their territory. Labradors living in the country rarely chase toys. They chase live animals. Jack Russells in the country don't scurry under beds, looking for treats. They chase actual rats in the woods.

I may not like the fact that these dogs are often unspayed or un-neutered, but they are still part of someone's family. And while many of the loose dogs I've seen in rural areas wore collars, I've never seen one with a tag stating the guardian's name and phone number. But taking these dogs is stealing them, not rescuing them. So if you're in the country and spot a lonely dog in a remote area, don't grab her unless that animal is in distress or is overly skinny, injured, or moving slowly as if dehydrated.

Another misconception: thinking that if you see a dog loose in the city, you should run after him. This may well cause him to take off—right into the street. When you spot a dog in a heavily trafficked area, you have to determine if your rescue attempt could cause injury or even death. When in doubt, for the dog's safety and yours, call animal control.

In situations where you decide it's safe to approach an urban dog and move toward him, pay attention to these cues: Are his ears up and alert? If they are low and back, he could be scared or aggressive. Does the hair on the dog's back stand up? That could also mean he is aggressive. Does he look at you, take a few steps forward, and give a low tail wag? That means the dog is happy and submissive; you can try to approach. A high tail wag means the dog is excited—but doesn't necessarily mean he wants you to grab him, so approach the dog calmly and casually. Avoid eye contact with the dog and approach in a normal walking posture.

As you approach, if the dog seems to be walking toward you, don't move in a direction that makes the dog have to cross traffic or venture anywhere that might be dangerous. If the dog stands still or looks scared, approach him so that if he suddenly moves away from you, he also moves away from traffic or other risks.

If the dog has a tag and a collar (and you can get close), take a photo of the tag. That way, even if the dog runs off, you can call the owner.

If you decide it's appropriate to touch the dog once you've reached him, start low, even down to a crouch, to appear in a submissive state. Hold your hand low and see if he will sniff it. If he does, give him some verbal praise and then lightly rub a finger against his nose to see how he reacts. If he stays motionless, stay still a while longer to see if the dog gains interest in you before trying again. A motionless dog staring at you might indicate he sees you as a threat, so don't push your luck. If the dog looks away or moves to sniff you, it's a better sign. If the situation feels safe, you can try to pet the dog.

Don't start over the dog's head. A dog can become scared if a human stands up and reaches over him—this can feel threatening, as a dog will stand over another dog to show dominance. Most dogs prefer to be touched on their sides rather than their head at first, but I've often found that if a stray is sniffing my hand and I start to lightly move my fingers, he will lean his head into my hand. If a stray does this, you can then try brushing your fingers against the dog's cheeks or chin. Hesitate slightly and give verbal praise. Many dogs will then take a step toward you to get more attention when the petting stops, indicating the dog trusts you. Pet him more. Otherwise, take it slow. If a dog doesn't lean into you when you touch him, it's a better idea to try petting his sides instead of his head.

If rescuing dogs is something you'd like to do, then carry a leash in your car at all times. But don't worry if you don't have one, because that's what shoelaces are for. I've brought many rescues home with one of my shoes falling off. To secure the shoelace to the dog, you'll have to get a hand on the dog's collar (if he has one). If he doesn't, you can always use the shoelace as a collar, placing it over and around the dog's neck once you have won his trust.

If the dog is wagging his tail, puts a paw on you, or presses his head into your body, you can try to pick the dog up or secure the leash. These are signs of trust, indicating he is happy to see you and accustomed to being around people. A pit bull once did this to me, so I opened up my truck door and he jumped in. He sat quietly in the passenger seat as if waiting for me to take him home.

To pick the dog up, start by putting one arm behind the dog's front legs and then placing that arm's hand around the top of the dog's neck in case he tries to bite. Gently push the neck down so that if he does bite, he might get your arm but not your face. Your other arm goes around the dog's body under the stomach.

If you can't pick up the dog, or if he backs away when you reach toward him, try to secure the leash or shoelace around the dog's collar or neck. Many dogs who act scared calm down once they are on a leash. They understand this means they are going for a walk. If the dog escaped, or something frightened him out of his yard and he is now lost, panic might set in. But if he feels a leash, he may well feel in control. He's just going for a walk, and every time he goes for a walk, he also goes back home. Just tie your shoelace around the dog's collar or neck as best you can while using your favorite calm doggy voice to reassure him.

Now you have control of the dog. If the dog walks with you, you can bring him home. If the dog doesn't want to walk with you, struggles, or is scared—or you are scared for your own safety—first lower yourself to the ground, so you aren't standing over the dog, and speak in a calm voice. If you fear the dog is going to bite you, look out for your safety and call animal control. But remember: If someone reports a dog to the authorities as a biter, that dog can be viewed as dangerous and is more likely to be put down.

If you can take the dog to your home, make sure he is secured in an area from which he can't escape. If the dog whines and looks out a door or gate often, it's a good sign he wants to be returned to his guardian. Don't be surprised, however, if the dog just reluctantly inspects his surroundings with a sigh and a "Now what?" expression.

If the dog has a tag, you're in luck. Otherwise, the sad truth is that it's unlikely the owner is looking for, or even wants, the dog. Dogs are abandoned for innumerable reasons, and people who keep their outside dogs permanently in their yards often don't care if the dog digs under the fence and manages to find freedom. Only about 15 to 20 percent of lost dogs are ever returned to their guardians.

That said, there's still a chance you can find the owner of a lost dog without a tag. First, check with neighbors in the area to see if they recognize the dog. This is the easiest step, and the most likely to work. Second, if you can get the dog to a vet, have the dog scanned for a microchip to obtain the owner's phone number. If that doesn't work, take a photo of the dog, call local veterinarians and shelters, and send them the picture or describe the dog to see if anyone recognizes him as a client and can locate the guardian.

Next, check websites such as Craigslist and Petfinder to search lost dog ads in and around your area. It's possible the dog has wandered quite a distance, which is why nobody in the area recognizes him. Also, consider posting ads online and in your neighborhood for the found dog. The best places to post these notices are at busy intersections, vets' offices, shelters, and pet supply stores. Even if the stray's guardian doesn't see the ad, someone who knows the stray dog might. Don't forget to include a contact number and picture so people familiar with the dog can immediately recognize him.

Janie and Buttons

Janie is the president of Wag 'N Wash, a full-service pet salon in New Jersey. Over the last two decades Janie has rescued countless dogs (and cats) from urban streets. Of all these dogs, she first thinks of Buttons, a fifteen-pound Jack Russell–West Highland terrier mix.

Many years ago Janie was working in a depressed area in northern New Jersey where, she says, "there wasn't a day that went by where someone didn't dump a dog in a nearby parking lot or where I didn't see a dog that had been run over or had been left to freeze to death during a winter storm." One Sunday, she received a call from a woman about a badly burnt Yorkie who had been left to die in a garbage can. Janie immediately drove the twenty miles down to the location and found a five-pound puppy (soon to be named Buttons) who'd been thrown in a tin garbage can after someone had poured battery acid over her tiny body. Janie cradled the dog in her arms, swaddling her in soft cotton to prevent chafing of the burns, and drove her to a local veterinarian. The doctor thought the severely malnourished dog was about five months old.

Buttons stayed in intensive care at the veterinary hospital until she was well enough to be cared for at home. The doctor said it was a miracle that she survived at all. The healing process was long and hard. Buttons had to take more than five rounds of antibiotics to combat the numerous infections in and on her little body. Taking care of her was a full-time job requiring three shifts a day to administer the medications as well as apply the herbal tinctures Janie used to soothe the burned areas.

After five weeks of home care, Janie introduced Buttons to her two other dogs (also rescues from the same area). Buttons was able to hobble a bit by then, and seemed elated to see other canine friends.

Janie had wanted to adopt Buttons out as she progressed in health and socialization. Unfortunately, when anyone came to meet her, she either hid or growled. She was extremely fearful of children and men, so Janie decided to add Buttons to her pack and worked hard to gain her trust. The reminders of her terrible start in life remained—many parts of her body were bald and blackened by the burns and scalding, but most of her hair eventually grew back in.

Buttons lived a long, happy life, always defensive with both adults and children but an inspiration to everyone who met her. And she gave Janie inspiration, too, helping her decide to open a dog-related business, where she could finally realize her lifelong passion of caring for dogs and giving back to the animal community.

Abused Dogs

Rescuing dogs from abusive situations is far different from a street rescue. For those not in law enforcement, there are no SOPs to follow that both ensure the safety of the person who has witnessed animal abuse and allow the witness to effectively help an abused dog.

The first step you should take if you see a dog who appears to be neglected is to snap some photographs and video footage of the animal. If you actually witness an act of abuse, it's important to obtain documentation, but don't let that prevent you from intervening in a timely manner. If someone is slapping or roughing up a dog in a way that won't cause visible injury, taking phone video footage is the only means of getting the abuser prosecuted because there won't be any physical evidence to prove that the dog was, in fact, abused. If you're the only witness, the police will need more than your word. Slapping, kicking, or throwing a dog when it's not a necessary form of self-defense against a violent dog is an act that causes "unnecessary suffering," common legal wording used to define animal cruelty in most states' statutes. If the abuser is causing physical damage to the dog, intervening immediately is necessary to prevent further harm. That physical damage is itself evidence, and in many states an act of abuse that results in an injury is a felony rather than a misdemeanor.

When in doubt, call the police. I cannot recommend people put themselves at risk, so calling for help is better than placing yourself in a dangerous situation. That said, I have to admit that there are very few places in the United States I've ever lived or worked where I felt confident that the local authorities would bother to do anything about someone neglecting or beating a dog. Without concrete evidence showing a pattern of abuse, most police officers to whom I've reported wouldn't bother to take action unless the abuse was especially horrific, or they were trained to know what to look for and were part of a specialized animal-cruelty unit. I'm not trying to blame or chastise law enforcement here. I'm simply speaking from almost two decades of experience.

Here are a couple of examples of what I've done when I've witnessed an abusive situation.

When I was twenty years old, I was living in an apartment complex in a southern Texas town and working in a no-kill shelter. My neighbors in the apartment next to mine were about my age, newly married, and had just bought a husky puppy from a pet store. The puppy was a hyper ball of brown and white fur who'd licked and bit at my hands while I first said hello to him. One day about a month after the neighbors bought him, when the puppy was twelve weeks old, I heard him shrieking through the wall of my apartment. I ran over to the neighbors' and pounded on the door. The young woman opened it. She looked embarrassed but said nothing.

"What's going on?" I asked.

She didn't respond

"Is the puppy okay?" I asked.

We looked over at the puppy cowering in the corner of the living room, facing away from us.

"He's being an ass and biting. So I kicked him," she finally said.

I don't remember what thoughts were going through my head, but I simply walked past her through the doorway, picked up the puppy, and said, "I'm taking the puppy. Don't ever do that shit again."

I then walked back into my apartment and prepared to have a puppy stay the night by removing items that could be a choking hazard, or that I didn't want damaged, from within the husky's reach. And as I always kept dry dog food on hand for any rescue I might come across, I made sure the puppy received some kibble as a treat to help alleviate his stress.

Later that night, the husband knocked on my door. He looked incensed but embarrassed. I got the impression that he wanted to punch me in the face. He also had the sense to know his wife had misbehaved.

"I know what she did was wrong, but don't ever talk to my wife like that," he said.

I took a breath, told him I wouldn't, and also promised that I wouldn't call the police. I told him that they probably weren't able to handle a puppy right now, but I would make sure he found a loving home by taking him to my shelter. The husband nodded, likely considering that while I was guilty of dognapping, his wife was guilty of cruelty to animals. He turned, walked away, and ended the final conversation I ever had with either of them.

On another occasion, while I was volunteering with Habitat for Humanity in Fayetteville, North Carolina, three volunteers and I were putting shingles on a roof when we heard a dog's shrill cries. By looking down, I could see over a wooden fence that someone was using a deflated bike tube to strike something with vicious whipping motions. The look on the man's face was one of rage. Every time the tube came down, I heard a dog cry out. The other volunteers simply shook their heads and kept working. I put down my hammer, climbed off the roof, and walked over to the home. After banging on the door long enough, I confronted the homeowner, who admitted he was distraught because his rottweiler had three puppies who were always digging in his yard. I composed myself when I realized I had been hearing puppies screaming rather than a single dog.

I explained to the man that his puppies seemed to be too much for him, that the other volunteers and I had seen what he had done, and that I worked with rescue groups and shelters across the state on a regular basis. My words were intended to make the man think he had angered the entire rescue community and to try to placate him into giving up his puppies. He agreed to hand them over. His only condition was that I didn't call the police. After waiting outside his front door, he returned shortly with the three twelve-week-old puppies, shaking and terrified. Dirty and bedraggled, they buried their heads in my chest when I held them. I placed the armful of puppies in my truck—and immediately called the police.

Because I hadn't seen the bike tube actually striking a puppy, but only the whipping motion, the police couldn't make an arrest. However, that same day I contacted a local no-kill shelter that could easily adopt out the puppies to much better homes than the one they had come from. Before the sun had set, the three puppies were taken in, bathed, vaccinated, fed, and given blankets and toys.

What Kind of Dog Do You Want?

What kind of dog to adopt depends heavily on your lifestyle, family, and the environment the dog will live in. Do not put too much stock in believing that certain types of breeds always have certain types of personalities. While Chihuahuas are often described as yappy, nervous dogs, I've known many who are calm and quiet. Pit bulls have a terrible reputation for being aggressive, but I've known countless pits who just wanted to cuddle with any stranger who comes their way. Dogs are individuals, and just as with people, a number of variables determine who they are and what kinds of personalities they have.

If you have small children, make sure the shelter workers feel any potential adoptee is comfortable around kids. Also avoid getting a small dog who kids could injure. Some children have no experience with dogs, so learning how to be a dog-friendly human via adopting a rat terrier is a bad idea. The poor little dog's bones probably won't tolerate kids' figuring out which kind of play is too rough.

Consider whether you, your partner, or roommates have allergies to dogs or will tolerate shedding. Make sure you know if there's a weight limit on dogs in your apartment complex and whether you'll have to pay a fee (sometimes flat, sometimes monthly) for having pets.

If you want a dog who loves to run and fetch, you should have a yard or frequent access to open space, such as a park. If you live in a high-rise apartment, a smaller terrier may be better for you. Terriers, whose instincts drive them to hunt and explore tight spaces, are often happy crawling under beds and into blankets. Golden retrievers likely won't find that as stimulating and should have more space to enjoy. Of course, I know a Great Dane who loves the apartment life, and Floyd is a terrier who loves charging across open fields, so pay attention to what shelter workers or foster guardians tell you about each dog's individual personality, which counts far more than the breed.

If you want a low-key dog who will basically be a couch potato, an older dog may be the best choice. You may hear some occasional snoring in the background, but the charm of old dogs who love to lie around while you binge-watch TV is unmatched. I fondly remember playing with my childhood dog, Scotty, when he was an energetic and mischievous puppy. But my best memories of him are as an older dog. He was just as mischievous, demanding of chips and popcorn, and bold in his attempts to crawl into tight spaces, like under my mom's carefully planted bushes. Yet when he slowed down, he also let us pet him longer, and he spent more time lounging with us in the living room. His soft, slow licks when we bent down to kiss his nose made his final years the ones I cherish most.

Whatever kind of dog you adopt, make sure you can offer a safe environment. Dogs who like to dig will need secured fences so they can't scurry beneath them. Dogs who can jump very high will need tall fences. Dogs who are particularly small need homes where they can't slip through the cracks of a gate and run off into the street. If you're not in a position to make changes to accommodate the kind of dog you want, adopt one who can remain safe where you already live.

Scotty was my childhood dog, who grew up with me as I became an adult. I learned compassion and empathy from him, but I cannot say I have mastered forgiveness and friendship as well as Scotty did.

BRINGING YOUR RESCUE DOG HOME

Before you bring your rescue home, make sure you have the necessary supplies on hand. Know that your pet will eventually get sick, injured, or have an accident in or near your home. Just like a human child, rescues can, and probably will, run into problems you can prepare for.

Supplies and Resources You Will Need

Microchip

Microchips are a critical way to keep your pet safe in the worst possible situation: when he is lost without his collar and picked up by somebody else. About the size of a grain of rice, microchips are embedded under your dog's skin between the shoulder blades and contain either the shelter's or your personal information so you can be contacted right away if your dog is lost and picked up by another shelter. If a neighbor finds your dog and has a veterinarian scan your dog for the chip, the vet can obtain your information as well. Most shelters will microchip your rescue (it's painless), but if your rescue is a stray from the street or was given to you by someone else, take the dog to a veterinarian to make sure he or she is chipped.

First-Aid Kit

Let's be real: At some point, for some reason, your pet is going to wreak havoc. It may be cute havoc that involves jumping into a pile of leaves you're about to bag, but it also might be the kind of havoc that involves your dog eating sugarless chewing gum and then your having to induce vomiting so he doesn't die. First-aid kits for dogs, available at pet stores, can contain a variety of equipment. At a minimum, make sure yours has gauze to stop bleeding in an emergency, hydrogen peroxide, and a syringe with no needle.

Canine Poison

Most people understand that dogs, like human teenagers, shouldn't be allowed to eat Tide Pods. But many common human foods, while seemingly innocent, are poisonous to dogs. Even small amounts can be lethal. Here's a list of just some of these dangerous foods.

1. Sugarless gum, mints, and candies often contain a sweetener called xylitol. A small amount of xylitol can cause a dangerous increase in a dog's blood sugar levels or even liver failure.
2. Cooked bones can break into sharp pieces when chewed.
3. Raw meat can contain salmonella and E. coli bacteria, which are dangerous not just to dogs but to you as well. Make sure any table scraps you give your dog are cooked.

4. Onion can cause anemia in dogs. Generally, onion will be harmful to a dog only in large amounts, but toxins from onions can build up over time, so it's a bad idea to feed your dog any food with onion in it.

5. Raisins and grapes are much more toxic to dogs than onion. Depending on the size of the dog, it's possible for a handful of grapes to be lethal.

6. Chocolate must be avoided as it contains theobromine, an alkaloid that humans can easily metabolize but dogs cannot, allowing it to build up to fatal levels. Chocolate's caffeine also causes canine hearts to race. Vomiting and seizing are obvious signs of chocolate poisoning. So is running around like the dog is on a caffeine high.

7. Macadamia nuts typically cause nonlethal poisoning to dogs, resulting in weakness, vomiting, fever, and tremors.

8. Most dogs are lactose intolerant, meaning their bodies can't produce an enzyme called lactase to break down the sugar molecules in milk. The result can be diarrhea and bad farts. Unless you want that in your living room, don't let your dog in on the yogurt or ice cream.

9. Human medicines are often dangerous for dogs, so don't give yours anything not prescribed or okayed by a vet. For example, ibuprofen and drugs with acetaminophen, such as Tylenol, can be fatal.

If your dog has swallowed something you are worried might be harmful, call your veterinarian. If your local vet's office is closed and doesn't take house calls, call an emergency vet. If you don't know of one, try the Pet Poison Helpline at (855) 764-7661. They charge fifty-nine dollars for the call, but that includes immediate advice on what to do for your pet as well as follow-up consultations.

If you can't reach someone and need to know if you should induce your dog to vomit, follow these guidelines: If your dog is unconscious or has already thrown up, don't induce vomiting. Also remember that some corrosive substances, such as drain cleaner, can cause damage to the esophagus when coming back up, as can sharp objects, which can also create a choking hazard. Don't induce vomiting then, either. But if your dog has ingested a poisonous substance, such as a toxic food or medicine, and it won't hurt the dog's esophagus coming back up, do so. The most common, and safest, method is hydrogen peroxide. Using a syringe (from your first-aid kit), shoot 5 cc of hydrogen peroxide into the dog's mouth for every 10 pounds of body weight (and make sure your dog is not standing on your nicest rug). If your dog doesn't vomit after using the appropriate amount of hydrogen peroxide, get him to an emergency vet right away.

Car Harness

A car harness secures your dog to a seat belt so when you slam into another car while texting someone about the new rescue you just adopted, your rescue doesn't go flying through the windshield. Some are simply straps that hook onto your dog's harness and connect it to the seat belt, while others are dog beds with stiff fabric walls surrounding them that hook into the seat belt.

Leashes

You'll need a leash for taking your dog off your property—and a few extras just in case one breaks or gets lost. There are two types: regular and adjustable. A regular leash is easier to pull on with two hands in an emergency, while adjustable leashes have the advantage of easily allowing you to keep your dog close when desired but also let you keep your dog at a distance. This is useful not only for letting your dog roam while remaining under control but also for some training purposes. Adjustable leashes do offer less control than regular leashes, but a small or older dog should be fine with one.

You may have to consider what kind of leash your dog prefers. Some dogs are frightened by the sound of adjustable leashes, while others have a seemingly uncontrollable habit of getting tangled in a regular leash. Toby, my cowriter Gene's rescue dog, is so terrified of the whooshing sound the adjustable leash makes that if he sees it, he immediately hides. But when the basic leash comes out, Toby jumps up and down in ecstasy. There is no one right leash for every dog. Experiment.

Always keep an extra leash or two on hand. Tragedy can occur when someone misplaces a leash and thinks it's okay to let his dog go pee near the street, just this once. The dog could run into traffic or spot a squirrel and take off running.

Collar and ID Tag

One goes with the other. Your pet's ID tag on his collar is the easiest way for people to contact you if they find your lost dog. It also makes it much more likely someone will stop to help your dog if he or she sees him wandering aimlessly on the street. A tag makes people realize your dog is a pet in need of assistance, and that helping your dog may simply involve one phone call and possibly keeping him in their car or yard until you arrive. Put the dog's name, your phone number, and your address on the tag.

When Disaster Strikes

A collar and tag can mean the difference between life and death. In 2005 after Hurricane Katrina hit, while I was rescuing dogs from abandoned homes in New Orleans with volunteers from Pasado's Safe Haven shelter, we found many dogs in severe distress. People who'd been rescued by soldiers and relief organizations weren't allowed to take their pets, and when we entered their homes, we often found the animals starving, running around whining and panicking. The shelter always tried to reunite the rescued dogs with their families, but that was often impossible if we had no way of knowing who had owned the house. Most dogs wore no collars or tags, and the houses contained no clues as to the owners' identity.

But in one home, the owners had prepared their dog for the worst, not only saving his life but making it easy for Pasado's Safe Haven to rescue him. When we entered the house, we found furniture scattered like debris throughout the rooms and a West Highland terrier mix pacing back and forth in the kitchen, barking. He had a forty-pound bag of dog food open on the counter so the floodwaters couldn't reach it and a couch nearby to climb onto to get to it. Water bowls covered the counter, so he could drink uncontaminated fresh water. He also had a leash around his neck, making it easy for us to walk up to him and get him under control.

As soon as I grabbed the leash, the dog stopped barking, feeling the pressure, and looked up at me through the matted, dirty white fur blocking most of his vision. The leash was connected to a collar, from which a small metal tag dangled containing the owners' names, address, and phone number, allowing the shelter to call them and assure them their dog had been saved and would soon be reunited with them.

Harness

Harnesses are better for walking your dog than collars because they don't put stress on your dog's neck and so won't choke your dog but at the same time offer more control than a collar.

Dog Bed

A dog bed is useful for giving your dog her own area where she can settle down and feel secure and comfortable. My parents' dog has a dog bed in the living room and another in their bedroom. My girlfriend and I have dog beds in the living room, bedroom, and car—having so many helps in case I find a stray dog and need to give him a quick, secure place to rest.

Crates, Pens, and Gates

Crates and pens are useful for house-training your rescue. An alternative is to keep your dog gated in one part of the house. Child gates are also handy for keeping your dog in or out of certain sections of your home.

Preventatives

Preventatives are medicines designed to protect your dog from parasites. They include dewormers, which protect against worms that can hurt your dog by living in his digestive system: roundworms, whipworms, tapeworms, and heartworms. All these worms can be fatal if untreated. Other preventatives repel ticks and fleas, which, besides inflicting painful bites, can cause anemia and carry fatal diseases.

Some preventatives are edible tablets; others are topical liquids.

The latter are placed on your dog's skin between the shoulder blades so your dog can't lick off the medicine before it can be absorbed into his bloodstream. Your vet, or the shelter from which you rescued your dog, can let you know which preventatives the dog will need.

Basic Grooming and Hygiene Supplies

At a minimum, you'll need shampoo, a brush, a nail trimmer, a toothbrush, toothpaste, and scissors. If you don't feel like trimming your dog's nails or brushing his teeth, your vet can do it for you, but make sure you have it done regularly enough that your dog's nails don't get so long they get caught in your curtains. Also check to see that plaque isn't building up on your rescue's teeth. Keeping a brush and scissors on hand lets you take care of mats in your rescue's fur before they develop. If you have a long-haired dog, regular brushing also helps you keep an eye on any sore spots, bug bites, or debris in your dog's fur that may otherwise go unnoticed. (If you prefer to use a professional groomer, you'll find it easy to choose one—more and more dog salons are sprouting up all over the country.)

Bathing and Brushing

About once a month, bathe your dog (more often if he enjoys running through creeks or rolling in mud puddles). Bathing dogs is easy, especially once your dog has grown accustomed to it. If your dog fears water, do not use a flooding technique; it may well make her panic as you try to force her to learn that the water is not a threat—which it will be if she is introduced to it too quickly. (Flooding techniques involve forcing a dog to endure something the dog fears, such as making a dog who is afraid of water stand in the stream of a water hose.)

Instead, gradually accustom your dog to being bathed, and learn to bathe the dog only when she's already calm. I have often started by putting warm water in a bucket or two and then taking the dog, water, and shampoo out to the yard. If you don't have a yard available, the bathtub is fine. Just make sure you have treats handy.

Much as you'll read in the section on training, the process is gradual. I recommend starting your dog's first bath by initially getting her to step into the tub or stand in place on the leash in the yard and then rewarding her with a treat. Next, put your hand in the water and start rubbing your dog as though you are giving her a massage. That deserves a small treat as well. Eventually, you can hold the water bucket up and splash a small amount of water onto the dog and offer another treat. Then, apply the shampoo and massage away. Receiving a shampoo massage is also a feat worthy of more treats. Remember to give constant praise to alleviate stress throughout the bathing process.

If I'm bathing a dog for the first time, I generally pour water onto her in handfuls. Shampoos are designed to be applied, rinsed off, and then reapplied to stand for a longer period before being rinsed off again. However, the first bath isn't an attempt to give your dog a luxurious coat so much as a chance to get your dog used to being bathed.

If the dog is feeling comfortable, you can try spraying the outdoor water hose directly on her at low pressure, which should feel good if it's hot outside. In a bathtub, try turning the bath faucet on at low pressure. You don't have to put your dog under the faucet if she's scared, but turning it on once she's calm, and giving her a treat and praising her immediately afterward, will help her to become accustomed to the sound of the faucet.

By the next bath, you may be able to speed up the process or position your dog closer to the faucet. Never force your dog to stay in the bathtub or under a hose if she is panicking. Slow integration, watching her body language and giving praise and treats as you go, is the best way to get her comfortable with baths. You want your dog to associate bath time with praise and comfort—not fear.

Brushing teeth is as important, if not more so, than bathing. Brush as often as possible to prevent plaque buildup and more serious issues. Ideally, brush your dog's teeth every day, but even if you only do it once a week, you're better than most people. Brushing doesn't have to be difficult for either of you, especially when you get your dog accustomed to the brush correctly. Finger brushes, which are bristled brushes that are hollow so you can fit your finger inside, are useful for cleaning dogs' teeth, but larger dogs may need a brush with a handle so you can reach the back molars. Always use dog toothpaste, since human toothpaste can be harmful to dogs' stomachs. Also, dog toothpaste is often flavored, making it enticing.

Just as with bathing, you want to start slowly with brushing. Choose a time when your dog is calm. Make sure your dog is comfortable with your touching her mouth and gums. Putting some peanut butter on your finger is an excellent way to get your dog accustomed to your finger in her mouth. Give a little of a flavored dog toothpaste to your dog like a treat. Then you can put some of the toothpaste on the brush and move the brush on your rescue's teeth just as you did with your finger.

Give constant praise to your dog to keep her relaxed and feeling rewarded for her amazing behavior of licking something off a brush. If your dog is comfortable with the process so far, lift her lips up and angle the brush forty-five degrees to brush the teeth and gums. If there's a little bit of bleeding from the gums, don't worry. That can be normal, although consistent or heavy bleeding could be a problem and you'll want to notify your vet.

Start with the teeth that are easiest to reach. If your dog gets very uncomfortable with the brush going too far back into her mouth at first, don't make the process traumatic for her. You can gradually work your way to the back of her mouth next time. After brushing, give a favorite treat and lots of praise.

Food and Water Bowls

Ceramic dishes for both food and water are the best choice—they are heavier and thus less likely to get knocked accidentally by an anxious dog sprinting toward a new meal. Also consider a set of collapsible dishes for when you take your dog on a hike or out to the park. These are usually made of rubber or fabric and can be flattened to save space and then popped out again to form a bowl.

Dog Food

The shelter or rescue from which you adopt or the vet who examines the stray dog you picked up can tell you what kind of food is best for your rescue based on the dog's age, size, and condition. Make sure to pick a dog food brand that doesn't use abusive food-trial tests on dogs, however (see page 224).

Sean and Bolt

Thirty-three-year-old Shaun Duling works in the DC area training employees at a natural-gas company. Prior to his current job,

Shaun served in the Marine Corps from 2003 to 2007 in Iraq and Afghanistan. After his military service ended, Shaun returned overseas in a civilian capacity as a contractor for a surveillance team.

Every time Shaun went overseas he would unofficially adopt one of the many wild dogs who were always hanging around the base. "Having a dog there made the deployment and desperation a little easier to deal with," Shaun says.

In September 2011, Shaun returned to Afghanistan, where his team was attached to the German army; he was one of six Americans on an all-German base. On his very first day at the base, Shaun spotted Bolt, a skittish, standoffish dog who watched the troops from afar. Bolt didn't look very healthy—a tan, white, and brown Anatolian shepherd, he was malnourished and underweight. But Shaun saw a lot of personality and soul in the dog's eyes and face, despite the rough life he'd led: The Afghan police who guarded the base's gate routinely threw rocks at him to keep him away. So Bolt kept his distance, and yet he never kept too far away, feeding on whatever scraps he could find.

Shaun was attracted to this sweet, underfed loner, and he started keeping an eye out for him. He'd put food out, trying to lure the dog in, but although Bolt came closer and closer, he never got near enough for Shaun to pet him. One day Bolt was attacked by some of the other wild dogs on base; Bolt was neither an alpha dog nor part of a larger pack. Shaun ran in and broke it up. Bolt, bleeding profusely, was so badly injured he couldn't walk. Shaun gingerly picked the dog up and brought him to his tent, where he found a box and placed a tarp over it and let Bolt sleep. Shaun had no medical training but did his best to cure the dog's wounds, which weren't as bad as Shaun had feared.

After a few days Bolt could stand again, and soon he could walk. After that, the human and the canine were inseparable. Shaun was working the night shift, from midnight to six a.m., so Bolt would wake up with Shaun at eleven thirty and follow him to Shaun's office, where the dog would curl up outside until work was over. No matter what Shaun did, Bolt followed.

For a while, all went well. Winter came with its harsh northern Afghanistan winds and twenty-below temperatures, and Shaun would often sneak the dog into his tent. Then, the following summer, the commander of the German base announced that every dog had to be thrown off the base. Special Forces dogs who were trained to sniff out explosives were about to arrive. The Germans couldn't risk one of the wild base dogs attacking these expensively trained military dogs.

Shaun was in a tough position: He and Bolt had bonded, but Shaun didn't want to risk his job. There wasn't anything he could do. So he said his goodbyes to Bolt. Shaun took off the collar he had braided Bolt out of paracord so he could remember his dear friend. He then loaded Bolt onto the back of a truck. Shaun said his heart broke.

The German army rounded up the dogs and drove them out to a village approximately twenty miles from the base, opened the doors, and all the dogs ran off—except Bolt. He wouldn't leave. The convoy started to return to base, and then some of the German soldiers saw Bolt running behind the truck. They didn't think much of it; they figured he'd get tired and give up. (Fortunately for Bolt, this was a military vehicle traveling over rough roads, so they weren't moving very fast.)

But Bolt didn't give up. Finally one of the vehicle commanders was so moved by the spectacle of this dog desperately trying to return to his friend that they stopped, let him on the truck, and drove him back to the base. After hearing the story, the commander agreed to let Bolt stay on the condition that Shaun start the paperwork to bring him back stateside.

Shaun hadn't thought this was possible, but now that he had an order, he got in touch with the English rescue organization Nowzad, which offered to help. The biggest issue would be getting Bolt from the base to Kabul. Unfortunately, Shaun was scheduled to leave before this could be arranged, but two of his friends offered to help out.

When the helicopter to pick Shaun up landed, he got in. But Bolt broke free from Shaun's friends and tried to jump into the Black Hawk with him. Shaun had to pick him up and carry him back. "I was just a mess at that point," Shaun says. "Tears were streaming down my face. I didn't know if I would see him again. Despite all the help, there was a strong chance he wouldn't make it to Kabul, or through the process of quarantine, neutering, and all the physical exams he would have to pass to prove he was healthy enough to come to the US."

But Shaun's friends were able to find a local Afghan who drove the dog through some very rough areas to the capital city, where Bolt passed all his medical tests. He was finally cleared to fly to America.

He arrived two months after Shaun had left.

Bolt had to be sedated to make the long trip from Kabul to Dubai and then to DC. When Shaun picked him up at the airport, Bolt was still sleepy and barely seemed to know what was happening. But slowly, after sniffing Shaun, he began to wag his tail, and the life came into his eyes. "It wasn't one of those crazy viral videos," Shaun says. "It was more like a progression of dead asleep to realizing, 'Oh, wow, it's you again.' This is one thing I really love about this dog. He was never really a hyper dog; he always had a mellow and relaxed attitude."

Shaun brought him home. Bolt transitioned seamlessly from being a wild dog in northern Afghanistan to a homebody in Virginia. Shaun worried that he'd have to be house-trained, that he'd chew up all the furniture while Shaun was at work, that he'd go nuts being alone. But Bolt was fine. "He has never once messed in the house, he's never chewed anything up, he never barks, he never gets into the trash," Shaun says.

"Most of all, given that Bolt had spent his life suffering through the hot summers and frigid winters of Afghanistan, he really just seemed to be content curled up on the couch next to me and out of the elements."

Toys

Most dogs love toys, but your dog's personality and background will determine how much he does, and which types of toys he likes. I've rescued dogs who have no idea what to do with toys, dogs who play with toys only if I'm involved, dogs who have a favorite toy, and dogs who like to have their toys rotated so they don't get bored with them. In general, it's a good idea to get a Kong brand toy. Kong toys are made of an extremely durable rubber and many are hollow inside, so you can fill them with solid treats or peanut butter, keeping your dog occupied for quite some time. They are wonderful as rewards. Most dogs also enjoy rope toys they can pull on with you—or one another. It's a good idea to try out anything your dog seems attracted to when you walk into the store. Let her look around and explore the toy aisle. If something grabs her attention, you may have a winner.

If you get your dog from a shelter, the staff may know exactly what types of toys your dog likes and how she likes to play with them. For example, you may need to keep tennis balls at the ready or break out the squeaky toys to keep her occupied.

Don't worry about breaking your budget. Some dogs love to play with objects as simple as sticks. My girlfriend's blind dog, Floyd, doesn't care much about keeping toys around, but if he smells a stick and you say, "Get the stick, Floyd!" a game of tug-of-war ensues. Floyd digs his tiny paws into the ground and positions his little potato-shaped body to pull vigorously against a stick bigger than he is. My parents' dog, Nick, on the other hand, enjoys toys that meet his more demanding and lavish lifestyle. A toy will keep his attention for about a week, after which he will grow weary of it and, spoiled prince that he is, turn to looking for treats instead of his old toy.

It was love at first sight when my parents met Nick at a shelter. Being veteran dog guardians, my parents give Nick the fulfilling duty of protecting their yard from deer and squirrels while rewarding him with frequent treats and constant love.

A Veterinarian

Your dog will need regular veterinary care. But before you entrust your pet to one, make sure you pick the best vet you can find. Most of us tend to select the closest one or one recommended by a friend or online review. It doesn't matter that your friend likes the vet, however. What's important is whether your friend's dog likes the vet. If your friend says his dog is terrified of going to the vet, that could be a sign that this person does not have a great bedside manner with animals.

Many welfare groups make lists of recommendations for finding a good vet. These typically include having a full range of equipment for treating emergencies, being on call twenty-four hours a day, and having an office close to your home. But there's more to a good veterinary practice than these practical considerations.

My experiences have taught me a great deal about what makes a good vet.

I've picked up a lot of dying, sick, or injured dogs while traveling across the world. Having a tight schedule to investigate puppy mills, factory farms, and slaughterhouses before the owners catch on and realize who I am, I seldom have time to waste. So when I've found dogs and puppies hit by cars or stumbling along the side of the road suffering from dehydration and mange, I've often needed to settle for the closest vet available.

What to Look for During a Visit to a Vet's Office

1. Pay attention to your dog's behavior. If she's terrified of going through the door, it could be a bad sign. Of course, some dogs are always scared when away from their homes, others are frightened of new places, and some others are frightened of other animals. Still, if you leave your rescue at the vet's for a few hours or overnight, pay attention to her body language when you return. A vet and the office staff should make sure they are comforting and providing enrichment to animals in their care. If they are, your dog will be like my parents' dog, who sprints through the door of the vet's office and then jumps on staff members to say hello.

2. Pay attention to the vet's staff. I once took a sick stray dog to a vet in Yucatán, Mexico. The poor boxer was skin and bones and

had mange, leaving her skin bloody and gray. As another investigator and I placed her on the exam table, a man sitting in the corner texting on his phone mumbled instructions to a vet tech before standing up, sighing, and asking us what we wanted him to do with our dog. That was a bad sign. Dog lovers (like me) tend to ignore new people and get excited about meeting a dog. A good vet should be a dog lover.

3. Your vet should immediately want to look at and interact with your dog, not just you. She should ask relevant questions about your rescue and show concern for your dog's health by asking about the dog's diet, medical history, personality, and where you got him.

4. Ask whether your vet either provides twenty-four-hour emergency care or can refer you to a place that does. Few veterinarians can be at their office at midnight, but yours should at least be able to let you know about emergency options in the area.

5. A good vet will be patient. Traveling in Hidalgo, Mexico, an investigator and I noticed a small dog wandering the side of the road, the thin rope around her neck dragging along the ground. We stopped the car and I scooped up the dog, who was basically a walking skeleton as she feebly tried to walk away from me. She must have weighed little more than eight pounds but looked as though she could grow to a plump twenty-five pounds when spoiled. I named her Rosita. The first vet we found barely looked at her, warning us not to wash the fleas off of her because the water could send her into shock. We decided to get a second opinion. The next vet not only gave more sane medical advice but also took the time to pet and comfort Rosita, ask where we found her and how she had behaved until we got to the vet's office, and where little Rosita was going to go afterward.

6. It's a sign of experience and professionalism if your vet wants to keep your dog overnight to monitor her and is willing to take a few minutes to soothe her fear before an examination. Rosita needed a vet's patience so she could calm down enough to take the medicine she needed for fleas, anemia, and dehydration. Shortly afterward, Rosita was adopted by local contacts and quickly ate her way to those plump twenty-five pounds.

7. A good vet will recommend spaying or neutering and microchipping your dog. If she doesn't, something is wrong. It's that simple.

GPS Tracker

If you plan to have your dog running off leash, a GPS tracker can help find her if she decides to dash out of sight. A variety of companies make GPS trackers that fit on your dog's collar. You can then track your pet with an app on your smartphone. Different trackers have different ranges. Some require monthly subscriptions; others don't. Some have battery lives of a few days; others last for months. Their range varies from several hundred feet to miles.

Spay/Neuter Surgery

You absolutely must consider spaying (female dogs) or neutering (male dogs). Spaying and neutering help prevent cancer and decrease the chance your dog will mark territory by peeing in your house or try to run away to find a mate. Of course, it also prevents your rescue from having puppies—there are already plenty to go around!

If you obtain your dog from a no-kill shelter, she is almost guaranteed to have already been fixed. But if your rescue is a stray you picked up off the street or comes from a municipal shelter that doesn't provide these surgeries, you may need to have your vet do it. The service almost always costs under $200; low-cost humane clinics can provide it for considerably less.

Dog-Proof Your House

Make sure that your home is safe for your rescue by following these steps.

Get or Secure Fences

If you have a yard, become familiar with the three most common ways dogs get lost: through loose gates, by digging holes, and by climbing chain-link fences.

Many strays will simply slip through fence gates that aren't well secured. If you can push the gate far enough to fit your foot through, your Chihuahua can do the same. If you can push your knee through the gate, your pit bull can squeeze through. If your dog is tall and energetic, like an Irish setter, you may need a fence five to six feet high. If your dog is a terrier, he may be prone to digging, so sink your fence several inches into the ground or place bricks or stones along its bottom. If you have a chain-link fence, keep an eye on your rescue to make sure she doesn't climb it. If you've never seen a dog do this, you may think I'm joking, but I've watched a Labrador, a poodle, and more mutts than I can name do it. Some dogs just have it in them. If this is the case, you'll either need a wooden fence or to make sure your dog isn't left unsupervised in the yard.

Remove or Store Poisonous Items

In addition to the foods noted earlier, make sure no medications are within reach of your rescue. Many plants can be poisonous to dogs as well, but the truth is that it's rare for dogs to eat houseplants, and what plants you have may depend on where you live. Still, to be extra safe, keep all plants away from puppies.

Remove Choking Hazards

Dogs rarely swallow hard objects that don't smell like food. In fact, I've never seen it happen. However, a bored dog—especially a curious puppy—may decide to chew on something that could lodge in his throat. So it's a good idea not to leave something like a hair tie or lighter lying around within reach when your dog will be left alone for a long time.

Pad or Remove Sharp Objects

If your rescue is old or has poor vision, there's an increased chance he may bump into sharp objects. Fireplace pokers and the edges of low furniture can be painful to stumble into. They are best removed or padded so your rescue doesn't hurt himself.

Install Appropriate Floorings

Older rescues may have trouble walking on polished wood or slick linoleum floorings. Carpet is better, but if that's not an option, throw rugs on which older dogs can take firm steps are a good option. Also, if the rescue has poor vision, feeling the different fabrics of different rugs will help her remember where she is and find her way around.

Alissa and Canela

Alissa Bushnell is a publicist who divides her time between her homes in Sonoma County, California, and southern Baja, north of Cabo San Lucas, Mexico. Alissa has been visiting Baja for many years, and in fact, sixteen years ago she met her husband in a bar in nearby Todos Santos. Alissa and her husband had thought about rescuing a dog for years, but because Mexico is so important to them, they decided that although it might be more difficult to rescue a dog in a foreign  country, a Mexican dog would mean a lot. And Mexico is filled with dogs who need rescue.

In La Paz, a group of dog lovers founded an organization called Baja Dogs La Paz, which is dedicated to "using a holistic approach that encompasses education, sterilization, community support programs to prevent abandonment, and rescue efforts." Every year on their annual visit to Todos Santos, Alissa and her family kept looking for the right dog to rescue but never quite found him or her until several years ago when Alissa's daughter, Sadie, who was nine at the time, said, "Look, if we're going to get a dog down here, give me your phone." Alissa did. Sadie then discovered the Baja Dogs La Paz website and said, "This is the one I want." She pointed to a photo of a young dog with cinnamon coloring who was named Canela, the Mexican word for "cinnamon," which is Sadie's favorite spice.

Canela is, Alissa thinks, a mixture of a black mouth cur and, because her fur is so soft, perhaps a Shar-Pei. Now fifty pounds, she was eleven when they first met her. Alissa went to work. They set up an appointment to meet Canela and immediately fell in love with her. They filled out the applications. Baja Dogs La Paz interviewed Alissa and her husband to make sure that they understood the responsibilities of rescuing a dog, as well as conducting a Face-Time "site visit" of their home in order to ensure the dog would be in a suitable environment. Once adoption was approved by Baja Dogs La Paz, they made sure Canela was spayed and her shots up to date. The organization provided them with a leash, a harness, and a crate to carry Canela back on the plane—they even checked with the airline to make sure the dog was an appropriate passenger. The biggest hurdle in international adoption is ensuring that the paperwork is filled out correctly and that the dog's health is good. Rabies shots are required for entry into the United States, and if you adopt a dog who is too young, you may not be able to get the shots. Luckily, Canela was old enough and her paperwork all came through.

Canela had been found in the desert by a Baja Dogs La Paz volunteer. Her mother had been spotted wandering around, dehydrated, but clearly nursing, so the volunteer gave her some water and then followed her back as she went to nurse her puppies. First the volunteer found two, then a few hours later two more, and then two more. Alissa says that in her experience, these Mexican rescue dogs, because they don't know where their next meal is coming from, don't tend to wander far from the home, so even though Alissa's house is on five acres, Canela never wanders more than a hundred yards away.

Creating a Dog Space

Your rescue dogs will quickly become a welcome part of your home—but make sure that just as you are ready for your dogs, your home is ready for them, too.

Spaces for Socialized Rescues

Your rescue will want her own space, but where this space is, and what it is, depends entirely on the dog. Friendly rescues, already accustomed to life in a home and acclimated to the sounds of electronic devices and the activity of people coming into and out of various rooms, may be comfortable with one dog bed in the living room and another in your bedroom. If the dog is very sociable, she'll probably want to be able to see you while you go about your normal activities.

Spaces for Frightened Rescues

If your dog was rescued from an abusive person, is a scared stray, or was rescued from a puppy mill, a dog crate where she can feel safe may provide a better option than a regular dog bed. If she is timid but somewhat interested in you, then leave the crate door open to give her the option of going inside. Keep the crate near an area where you normally spend time to help the dog become used to you.

If the rescue is afraid of you, leave the crate door open, but put it in a dog pen or another blocked-off area. This keeps the dog relatively confined and unable to run off in fear but doesn't force her to rely on feeling safe only in an enclosed area like a breeding cage.

Make Your Dog Comfortable

Your rescue may never have known what comfort is. Here is your chance to really shine as a rescuer.

Making Socialized Rescues Comfortable

If your dog came from a shelter or is immediately happy to be taken in off the street, shower him in praise, petting, and treats. You are a loving guardian, and living with you means winning the dog lottery. Make sure your rescue knows it! You can set boundaries for your dog, of course, such as keeping him out of certain rooms or forbidding him from jumping up on counters, but remember to reassure him by your actions that he no longer has to worry about limited bathroom breaks or to beg frantically for attention.

Making Frightened Rescues Comfortable

If your rescue is scared (but not to the point of running away from you or barking in fear), you'll want to spend plenty of time with her, making sure that when she lets you pet her, she gets a small treat. If your rescue often looks away from you, petting her and then stopping will likely make her turn toward you slightly. When she does that, make sure she gets another treat and plenty of praise. Repeat this process, which essentially teaches the rescue that paying attention to you means rewards.

For a rescue who fears your even looking at her, you may have to be patient and hold off on showering her with hugs and kisses. Emma, the Chihuahua I rescued from a puppy mill, and Daisy, the stray I rescued from a busy intersection, needed to learn that they had nothing to fear from me. I earned their trust by giving them space and not paying constant attention to them, allowing them to relax and not become startled if I walked by.

If your rescue is too scared to approach you and doesn't want to be petted, avoid even looking at her until you notice that she doesn't try to move away from you or jump up when you enter the room. Then you can look at her and say some words of praise, but don't linger. This teaches her that having your attention doesn't mean that she has to spend all her time with you—whom she may view as a danger—giving her a needed sense of freedom.

Once you notice that your rescue is looking at you on her own, you can focus on her for longer periods. If you can get close enough to leave a treat so that it's obvious you're doing it for her, go ahead, but only when her attention is focused on you, even if it's just a glance. You can continue this process as the rescue pays more and more attention to you, receiving more praise and treats for getting close to you and letting you pet her.

This process can take time. Remember that the rescue's comfort is more important than the satisfaction you seek from snuggling a dog. Your satisfaction comes from having saved a life. The cuddles will come later.

Set a Schedule (and Dog Chores)

The first thing you need to have at the ready for your rescue is time and the ability to set a regular schedule. You'll need to review all the things you do during the day to make sure you'll have time to take your dog out in the morning, go for walks, and spend time together in the evenings. When your rescue first arrives at your home, ideally you should plan to take a few days off to spend with your new dog. The weekend is perfect for this if you work regular business hours.

Consider how flexible your schedule is, and how much time you can spare to meet your dog's sometimes unexpected needs. I've learned this lesson by taking in strays of all ages and energy levels. Once I found a tall, lean, wire-haired mutt with the face of a terrier and body of a greyhound wandering the streets of a suburban neighborhood. She was mostly tan, so I named her Sandy. After unsuccessful efforts to find her owner, I contacted several no-kill shelters and told them I would foster Sandy until a placement opened up.

My life changed over the next month. Sandy was young and extremely spirited: She had lots of energy to burn. She wanted not just a morning walk and an evening walk but a morning and evening run. Not a jog. A run. For a mile and a half, twice a day, Sandy and I would dash through the woods at a pace that left me struggling for breath and my arm pulled almost out of its socket from trying to hold her on the leash. At the end of our workout, she was beaming with excitement. She seemed to feel much better doing something she was used to, even if a stranger was doing it with her. My taking the time to participate in these routine runs kept her happy, and we never had any problems with her peeing inside, barking, or chewing on anything in the house.

For most of you, Sandy wouldn't be the right dog. But you'll need to be prepared for the dog who is.

Your rescue will become more relaxed when he knows that he can predict when he'll be fed and walked, the times of the day that he gets a special treat, and when he gets to go on errands with you. A morning routine of eating, going outside to the "bathroom," and sniffing around some grass is an excellent way for a dog to start the day. An evening walk followed by feeding and then lounging around the couch is a great nightly routine.

Also set up "dog chores." For instance, if you have a yard, let your dog check the mail with you. For you, it's a boring task, but for your rescue the mailbox is an important place to sniff and mark. If you have an errand to run at a store where dogs are allowed, take him along—new territory, praise from strangers, and a ride in the car can make a dog's day!

Kate and BooBoo

Kate LaSala calls herself a dog advocate, rescuer, and transporter, as well as a certified dog trainer. To do all this, she spends a lot of time networking. In early June 2011, while perusing a rescue page, she saw a desperate plea for a dog who needed rescuing in rural Kentucky. BooBoo was one of fifty-two dogs living on the property of an Iraq War veteran named Kristie who suffered with severe PTSD. To help alleviate some of her symptoms, Kristie had volunteered with a local town shelter.

Kristie found tremendous comfort in helping the dogs in various capacities, such as running transport for the shelter, trapping ferals, and fostering dogs. But eventually she took in too many dogs, morphing from an accidental rescuer to a hoarder. She genuinely wanted to help these animals but became overwhelmed with all the work involved. Then, she was diagnosed with cancer, and so the plea for rescue.

Kate and her husband, John, decided to bring BooBoo to their home in New Jersey. Kate contacted Eleventh Hour Rescue (EHR) in Randolph, New Jersey, from which they had adopted their other dog. With EHR's help, Kate and John coordinated transport to get BooBoo from Kentucky to New Jersey. (EHR agreed to take in ten other dogs from the property, including BooBoo's three brothers and one sister.)

Finally, after weeks of working out transport details, dealing with interstate health certificates, medical clearances, lining up fosters, and everything else that needed to be done, they arrived to pick up BooBoo. The transport van showed up, and the driver took her crate out, opened the door, grabbed BooBoo's collar— and it broke. BooBoo escaped into a heavily wooded area off the side of a four-lane highway. A semi-feral black dog was now lost in New Jersey after enduring a seventeen-hour transport. Kate's heart sank; she doubted she would ever find BooBoo alive.

For the next nine days they searched exhaustively, launching a Facebook page, gathering an army of volunteers, posting a thousand flyers. Word was getting out, and Kate heard of many sightings, but BooBoo was so terrified that every time she saw someone, she would bolt. Running out of time, Kate decided to use one of BooBoo's brothers, Blaze, as a lure. They set up Blaze in a fenced courtyard tethered by a long cable tie line, and waited. Around two a.m., he started whining. As Kate walked away from him, BooBoo ran out of the woods to check on Blaze. Once BooBoo was safely in the fenced courtyard, John jumped out of the car, where he had been quietly sitting, and he closed the gate behind her.

When BooBoo was finally home, Kate discovered she had many fear-related issues—the dog was very scared of loud noises and had trouble relating to humans. But with a lot of love, force-free training, and patience, she blossomed. BooBoo eventually helped Kate and John foster over fifty more dogs, and three and a half years after being rescued, BooBoo received an AKC Canine Good Citizenship award and was certified as a therapy dog—she visits patients in hospitals, nursing homes, and schools to lift their spirits.

TRAINING

House-Training

House-training is the process of teaching your dog not to use the interior of your home as a bathroom but to go outdoors instead. As with all training, your dog's success at this process depends on you, the dog's guardian. House-training is not a series of commands that your dog can learn in a single training session, though. Rather, it's a process that begins the moment you bring your rescue home and involves creating and continuing good habits so you and your dog can ensure there's never an accident in the house.

House-training can be outlined in three stages, as described on the following pages.

First Stage: The Ride Home

If the rescue is coming directly from a shelter or is a stray you have picked up who is not panicked, put the dog on a leash when you first exit the car and let her walk around outside before taking her indoors. Remain calm and move slowly, letting the dog know you aren't expecting anything of her and allowing her to focus on her surroundings instead of on you. If people are talking to the dog or crowding her, or traffic is blazing by a nearby road, the dog will be distracted. For these reasons the backyard is better than the front of a residence.

At an apartment complex, choose an area away from a road or parking lot. If you live in a high-rise with nothing outside but a concrete sidewalk next to loud motor and foot traffic, find a nearby park where you can stop before going home from your walk. Dogs associate where to pee with the tactile sensation on their paws. If you want the dog to pee on grass, take her to some type of green space.

If the dog is a stray or was just rescued from an abusive situation and is too scared to focus on calmly sniffing grass, skip this step. The most important thing is for the dog to understand she is safe. This dog should go straight home, away from loud noises or unexpected attention that might overwhelm her, and into a room with food, water, and your calm presence nearby.

If possible, give your new dog access to only part of your home. You don't want her to become overly interested in all the new smells, or she could easily slip out of sight to go mark her new territory by peeing on it. It's best to let her have access to one room at a time, introducing her to other rooms on a leash either during the first day or a few days later. A calm dog can be trusted to see more of the house, whereas fearful or overly excited dogs should be given less area to explore so you can keep an eye on them. A fearful dog also shouldn't be pulled around on a leash. Rather than chasing her out of off-limit rooms, it's best to shut those rooms' doors so she can become comfortable with you and the new environment a bit at a time.

Second Stage: Early Days

Whether he is a puppy or an adult dog, your new rescue will need to go out often for the first few days or weeks before he begins to understand that indoors is his living space and outdoors is for urinating and defecating. Dogs pick this up naturally but need to be taught which is which. Mother dogs living outdoors, for example, will take their pups out of an enclosed den and lick them when they poop and pee outside as a reward for good behavior. The pups soon realize the den is not the bathroom.

Dogs raised in puppy mills generally learn to relieve themselves on the wire flooring of their outdoor cage rather than on the hard surface of their indoor enclosure. When rescued and placed in a home, these dogs need to learn which tactile sensation to associate with going to the bathroom once they no longer have cage wire beneath their paws.

Other puppy mill dogs have been kept in dog runs with concrete floors or another type of solid surface. They learn to go anywhere that is not the doghouse that serves as their shelter from the rain, cold, and heat. These dogs understand they shouldn't poop on their dog bed, but they consider the rest of the area fair game.

For these reasons, it's very important to keep an eye on your rescue and the messages she is giving you early on. If your dog begins sniffing the ground, circling, or is lying down and suddenly gets up and starts wandering nowhere in particular, you are seeing signs that your dog wants to do her business. Don't wait: Take her outside. When in doubt, trust your instincts and err on the side of taking your rescue out too often instead of too seldom. Most dogs can hold their bladder for up to eight hours, and some even more, but you shouldn't force your dog to do so if you can take her out more frequently. After all, you can probably hold your bladder for up to twelve hours in an emergency, but you don't want to and neither does your dog.

Every time your rescue goes to the bathroom outside, give her a treat and/or lots of praise. This is the time to immediately and without hesitation show the dog you are pleased. She will learn to associate the feeling of grass or earth with the correct place to go and will know that it pleases you.

Another house-training option is to place your rescue in a crate at night. This is a very common and popular practice that most experts and shelters recommend. (However, I admittedly did not always do this—remember, SOP does not necessarily apply!)

Dog crates are used to keep a dog in an enclosed environment overnight while you're sleeping. As explained earlier, puppies learn from their mothers not to use their den as a bathroom. The crate offers a space just big enough for the dog to move around, so she feels she is in a den she doesn't want to soil. She will then learn to hold her bladder before you take her out in the morning. Depending on the dog or puppy, crate training could take a few days, weeks, or months. If the dog has an accident in the crate, don't give any type of punishment or positive reinforcement. Simply take the dog outside and provide treats and praise if she pees where she's supposed to.

Some dogs will be familiar and comfortable with crates and will readily go into them. Other dogs need a little coaching. For the latter, help the dog to feel comfortable around the crate first. As with most training, remember to control the dog's environment by clearing the area of distracting noises, people, and smells. The dog should be able to focus only on you.

If you have a very high-energy dog who can't seem to focus on the crate and is jumping all around you looking for treats, exercise the dog beforehand. As with other training, remember that dogs have to expend physical energy before they can focus mental energy.

Place the crate in a quiet place, and when the dog approaches it, give her a treat. Next, place treats inside the crate, wait until she enters it, and then give her a few more treats as you shut the door. You can then give her another treat and walk away a couple of paces. Then leave the room momentarily, return, and give her a treat. Continue this process, leaving for progressively longer periods of time.

Don't give praise or treats if the rescue cries out as you leave. If she does, come back into the room calmly. Once the dog quiets down, give her a treat and restart the training process. Take baby steps. Some dogs learn to tolerate crating right away; others need days or longer.

Depending on how your dog does while crated, you may be able to situate the crate in your bedroom. If the dog is too noisy while you're trying to sleep, you may have to put the crate in another room.

Once the dog has been accident-free for two to four weeks, you can try substituting a dog bed for the crate. Just make sure you let the dog out to go to the bathroom right before going to bed and again when you get up. Don't make the rescue have to hold her bladder and start to fear she'll have to tolerate pain for too long. Some trainers recommend you take a dog out in the morning only after you've started your own routine so as to get the dog to learn patience. I disagree with this kind of training, as it might cause anxiety for the dog, whose comfort you should value as much as your own.

While these steps will work with many dogs, other dogs hate crates because they associate them with trauma. Many small-breed puppy mill dogs, for example, have spent so much time confined in cages that they will resort to spinning and barking behavior when inside a crate. You'll see their behavior change quickly from calm to panicky—wanting to snuggle one minute and circling and panting the next. If a crate makes your rescue act aggressively or fearfully, or if she begins to rely on the crate to feel secure, it likely isn't the best option. Consider something else: a collapsible pen.

Collapsible pens are gated walls that can be connected and used to form a square or circular enclosure. They come in various sizes and are generally used to keep animals confined to a limited area, such as on a tiled or laminated floor where they won't damage carpet or wood if they pee during the night. These pens allow rescues who might be traumatized by tight spaces to feel freer and to see more of their surroundings.

If you live in a high-rise apartment, you may opt for absorbent pee pads or old newspapers on which the dog can go if you can't get her out of the apartment quickly enough. Pads or papers are not ideal, but they are an acceptable option for people who are gone during the day. A better choice is to ask a friend or professional dog walker to take your dog out during business hours. Not only does the opportunity to go outside help with house-training, but by giving her more exercise it helps alleviate any stress and boredom your rescue might feel.

If your dog does soil your home, do not punish her. Simply clean up the mess, deodorize the area, and keep a careful eye on her so you can take her outside if she appears to need to go. Punishment confuses the dog, who doesn't understand what she did wrong. Remember that the proper tools for training are patience, persistence, and positive reinforcement (more about this later). If you have a new dog, you will probably have accidents in your home. Give your rescue time to learn the rules. Don't be afraid to take training back to basics and start over if she's not catching on. Always focus on positive reinforcement for wanted behavior, which increases the bond with your dog, rather than punishment, which will make your dog afraid of you.

Jill and Eddie

Jill Robinson is the founder of Animals Asia, a Hong Kong–based charity that seeks to end cruelty to animals in Asia. She has rescued many different animals from many different situations, but the one who will always stand out is Eddie.

Many years ago, Jill and a friend were visiting a live-animal market in China—places Jill finds "so hideous it's hard to describe their horrors to anyone who's not there. It's one of the most gruesome and grisly scenes on the planet." Mixed together are wild and domestic animals, and for the dogs it can be especially hard because many of them were stolen from their homes. They once knew humans as friends, but now they were peering at them from behind bars. All around them, other animals were being slaughtered in the most brutal ways possible. Most of these dogs were brought to the market in the backs of trucks in cages piled as many as ten high. They have no food, no water, and are simply thrown off the truck onto the concrete floor below. Some live; many die.

That day, as Jill was walking around the market, she was overcome with the impulse to save at least one of these unfortunate canines. Her heart bled for all of them, but her friend pointed to one dog in particular who, unlike the other dogs, all barking and crying, was lying in his cage quietly. When Jill leaned over, the dog licked her hand. That did it. Within a few minutes she was bartering to save his life—eventually settling for fifteen dollars.

Jill brought the dog to Hong Kong, where he had to go into quarantine for four months (although first it was a night in a Chinese hotel, where the dog dined on steak—a far cry from his earlier meals). It was during this time that the dog got his name from an Animal Asia supporter with a very dark sense of humor: Eddie, as in *edible*. (Roughly twenty million dogs are slaughtered for their meat each year in China.)

Eddie turned out to be exactly what Jill had hoped. He was fun, happy, loyal. She already had eight other rescues, but Eddie embedded himself into the pack almost immediately as its leader—he was, she says, a small dog with a big attitude. His best friend became Big, a rescued Newfoundland who was about six times Eddie's size. The two were inseparable, and Big would obediently wait his turn until Eddie had finished scrounging all the treats, never minding that his small pal had pilfered everyone's share.

Eventually Eddie became a dog ambassador in an animal therapy program in Hong Kong called Dr Dog. Jill had begun this program in 1991 to help the community connect with dogs who were victims of horrific treatment in Asia—from pedigree pooches abandoned on the streets once they were no longer in vogue to mutts seen as food for the table. The canine consultants and their volunteer companions would visit hospitals, disabled centers, and homes for the blind, deaf, orphaned, and elderly, demonstrating the comfort that humans can find from canine love.

Eddie was not the best Dr Dog. He constantly tested the nurses' patience—peeing onto potted plants inside the hospital wards, scrounging breakfast dim sum from the bedridden, slipping his lead and gaily trotting out of the ward with a desperate Jill behind him—but his dogged determination to make everyone laugh always won over hearts, except, perhaps, those of the cleaners. Eddie lived on for another thirteen years, relishing his role as a Dr Dog ambassador in which he was constantly hugged by Chinese celebrities and received an endless series of scratches and pats in return for anything edible he could sniff out from people's bags.

Third Stage: Continuing Good Habits

Just as with people, dogs can fall back into unwanted behaviors. A change in environment or a new addition to the family can create enough stress to cause a dog to mark territory or become too anxious to wait to go to the bathroom. Don't worry; it's temporary. Go back to crate- or pen-training basics if you have to. Most of the time, you'll simply have to remember to let your dog out frequently, praise her often when she goes to the bathroom outside, and make sure you are exercising her often so she can both expend physical energy and solidify her bond with you.

Territory Marking

If you've moved into a new home and your dog starts peeing inside, it's possible she has a health issue such as a urinary tract infection or kidney disease. Mention this behavior to your vet so you can rule out health concerns before assuming your dog is enjoying using your new rug as a bathroom.

It's also possible that stress or boredom is causing your dog to mark territory indoors. For a bored dog, negative attention is still attention, which is what your dog might well be craving. Besides making sure to take your rescue out often, take time to play with her and go on walks. Your rescue may have energy that needs to be burned off, so set a routine to make sure your dog is engaged in physical activity each day.

If your rescue is already physically active, she may be frustrated by a lack of mental stimulation. Training her to respond to some basic commands can help with this type of boredom by getting your dog to focus on and spend more time with you during her training sessions. (For information on teaching commands, see page 208.)

To Train or Not to Train (The Other Kind of Training)

Now that your rescue is home, you may decide to hire a trainer. Training a dog is useful for correcting some specific behavioral problems and for mentally stimulating your dog. It can also strengthen the bond between you and your dog. But not all dogs need training. Whether your dog does depends on not only him but also you.

Consider my parents' dog, Nick. Nick loves attention. When my parents first took him in, Nick would jump onto me, bouncing up and down like a yo-yo whenever I hugged my parents. A professional trainer told them this was bad behavior and that Nick needed to learn to sit still so he didn't interfere with my parents' desire that he learn to greet guests calmly. After the training, the next time I visited my parents, Nick sat and stared at me intently, seemingly about to explode from anxiety. When it was finally his turn to say hello, he shot like a rocket to my side.

Eventually, after I had spent months away working, I came back to town again to visit my parents. It was soon clear that they had decided Nick had every right to become excited when company came. Now when they see me pull into the driveway, they say my name, let Nick dash to the door, and when I step out of my truck, they open the door so Nick can charge me. I give him a huge hug while his tail slaps my arms and legs, and then we run around the yard until we're both out of breath. My parents don't care if that's not the kind of behavior their trainer wanted for Nick. That's the kind of dog they have, and they just love to see him happy.

If you don't care if your dog sleeps on the couch, hangs out around the dinner table, or lies on people's laps while they're watching TV, then don't alter those behaviors. Behavior only has to be altered if it's dangerous to you, a family member, or another animal in your household.

Key Training Concepts

Basic training provides a way for your dog to learn to trust you and follow your instructions. The key elements of successful training include a bond with your dog, exercise, a controlled environment, positive reinforcement, incremental steps, and persistence.

This kind of bond, as I mentioned earlier, will help your dog trust you and focus on you during the training process. You may find that you need to allow some time for your dog to settle into a routine and get to know you better before you can start training.

Exercise, including walking and play, will fortify your mutual bond and is critical for your dog's physical and mental health. Dogs are generally curious and fun-loving. They should be allowed to explore sights, sounds, and smells on walks and to play with you often, especially before training sessions. This helps dogs to expend energy so they can be more focused on the training.

A controlled environment is a place with limited distractions, again so your rescue can focus on you. For example, if you're in a park trying to teach your dog to sit for the first time, it's best not to have other dogs and people running around. Your living room may be a better location.

Positive reinforcement is the best way to motivate your dog. You'll want to provide ample treats to your rescue—as well as a lot of praise—as rewards during training. It's best if you use dog treats broken up into little pieces or small pieces of dog kibble. Treats are to be given out as the dog works toward a desired behavior. Once that behavior is achieved, you can give your dog a bigger treat or lots of praise to signify he has done particularly well.

It's also a good idea to switch between praise and treats once your dog has started to display a desired behavior in training. Then treats should come only randomly. This process helps your rescue learn that while he won't get treats every time he behaves, treats will come eventually, making the dog more likely to perform the desired behavior on command.

Incremental steps are behaviors that are even just slightly similar to the desired action. When you train your dog, remember to reward him for each incremental step he takes.

Persistence is also required. Sometimes training happens quickly, sometimes slowly, and sometimes progress is lost and has to be recovered. Usually, training for a specific behavior requires several sessions every day, with the length of the training depending on the dog and the behavior you desire to teach or correct.

For many unwanted behaviors, regular exercise, along with creating and reinforcing a bond between you and your dog, will usually solve the problem. For example, if your dog is chewing on your shoes or furniture, he is likely acting out of boredom and frustration. Exercise will help the dog vent energy. Exercise can also help reduce play-biting. Playing with your dog is a way to help fix the problem as it occurs. Whenever your dog bites at your hands, focus on putting a toy in his mouth. When your dog takes the toy, give him lots of praise in your most ridiculous cute-dog voice. Your dog will soon learn that toys, not your hands, are the desired objects to chew on.

Having a routine of various daily tasks will give the dog a sense of purpose and friendship with you. Being able to anticipate normal events such as feeding times and trips to the bathroom will help your rescue lose anxiety over such issues. Give your rescue moments to anticipate and look forward to, and you'll see that behaviors like chewing and even peeing in the house will decrease.

Regular exercise and a strong bond are much more useful than scolding your rescue for unwanted behavior. Scolding only increases anxiety, which adds to the problem. Good relationships with rescues are built on trust and love, not fear and punishment. Many people may want to punish a dog for an unwanted behavior but do so only after the dog has already peed on the carpet or chewed up a shoe. If the punishment comes after and not during the offending action, the dog won't associate the punishment with that action. Even if the punishment is given during the unwanted behavior, it may exacerbate the problem. As mentioned, much unwanted behavior occurs because a dog is frustrated from a lack of attention. Punishment only serves to provide that attention, even if it's negative attention. Always focus on rewards, not punishment, to achieve the behavior you seek.

Also important: Always remain calm yet assertive as you work to change your dog's behavior. If you find yourself becoming agitated or upset, take a break. Your dog will notice your anxiety and become more anxious herself. She should read your body language and facial expressions as calm and happy.

Hiring a Trainer

A good dog trainer should help you better understand your dog and help her with any specific behavioral issue that may be problematic—behaviors you can't, or don't want to, address by yourself. In the process, training will help your dog to feel more fulfilled and happier. That's what a dog trainer *should* do. Some dog trainers limit themselves to simply teaching specific behaviors. That is not the kind of trainer I recommend. If a trainer doesn't understand you, your dog, and what you need from your relationship as a family, the training won't be useful.

A wide range of expert opinion exists over which training methods are best—and some are at odds with one another. Some professionals believe that it's critical to establish the dog's human guardian as the most important member of the pack, and that his or her schedule and desires are most important. Others believe the purpose of training is to make sure that the dog and guardian can lead fulfilling lives together without one feeling dominated by the other.

I belong to the latter group. I never wanted a dog to be a second-class family member in my life. I wanted the dog to be considered an equal member. While always recognizing that our first family dog, Scotty, had no ability to communicate his concerns directly and was dependent upon us for everything vital to leading a good life, we never took advantage of this reality by making Scotty feel he was subservient to us. I also bring this mentality to how I treat rescue dogs in my home and which training methods I employ. I firmly believe that to train well, the dog must feel safe and satisfied, knowing that she is a valued family member. This means that before your dog is going to want to heel on a leash or roll over for a treat, she must feel comfortable with you.

That's why positive reinforcement is so important: It cements a loving bond. I avoid using any type of training technique that involves dominating a dog or flooding. Domination training creates the desired behavior by making a dog feel submissive to you. Flooding techniques, mentioned earlier, can create more fear than obedience. I've always been able to safely alter a dog's negative behavior(s) without resorting to these methods.

When looking for a good trainer, make sure the person you're considering understands these concepts. She should ask questions about your schedule, your dog's habits and personality, and not just what you want but *why* you want it. She will help you understand that your own habits must include a willingness to be vigilant and consistent with your own training. She will focus on positive reinforcement, will never punish dogs for unwanted behavior (including using choke chains or shock collars), and will take individual personalities into account.

Remember my parents' dog, Nick, who was jumping on company the moment they entered the house? My parents once took him in for training at a PetSmart store. The trainer there held group sessions with more than a dozen dogs per session. The same training techniques were applied in the same manner and at the same time intervals with all the dogs. While people were learning to get their dogs to heel, Nick's leash became entangled in a store display, eventually crashing it to the floor. Nick freaked out and charged through the aisles in a panic while dragging along remnants of the display until my parents could catch him. The trainer responded by putting Nick back in place with the other dogs and repeating the same techniques at the same time intervals.

I felt this was a mistake. The trainer should have first calmed Nick down and then gradually brought him back into the practice of heeling, giving him a steady supply of treats for his attempts. Instead, Nick was pushed back into line with his heart pounding, his mind consumed with fear of collapsing product displays instead of getting a dog treat. It took a while before Nick could see a harness again without quaking in fear.

A good trainer also knows that the most important factor in effective dog training is—you guessed it—exercise, and lots of it. Dogs should be exercised at least once a day and always before training sessions begin. However, many dogs need exercise multiple times a day and will want playtime in addition to one or more walks before they're fully able to focus. Depending on your lifestyle, you may need a friend or dog walker to help your dog get daily exercise. However, it's always best if you participate. Exercising with your dog helps create a bond that makes training easier, because the stronger the bond you create, the more your dog will want to please you and learn what to expect from your cues. This doesn't mean you should avoid having friends, family, and hired professionals help look after your dog if you don't have time. Just because your friend walks your dog while you're at work doesn't mean your dog won't listen to you. It just means that if you have the option of going home on your lunch break to walk your dog, it's better than having a friend do it.

Nicole and Maggie

Nicole Martel works as an administrative assistant in Winnipeg, Manitoba, where she has rescued four dogs. Her newest, Maggie, came about when her last beloved rescue died. Nicole had had a difficult time finding a new dog. Nicole explains that too often when you go online and find a dog you really like, she's gone when you show up. Finally, she called her cousin Glenn Sinclair, a large-animal vet just outside Winnipeg.  Glenn, with a wide circle of vet and rescue contacts, connected Nicole with a woman who in turn gave her the name of a man who travels to northern Manitoba communities to help them care for their canine friends—for example, how to build doghouses so that the animals have somewhere warm to seek shelter in the winter. He then connected Nicole to a teacher living on a nearby reservation and who had a terrier for whom she wanted to find a good home. Life is generally unbearable for stray dogs in these communities, as they have to cope with long and bitterly cold winters, and worse, many of the residents consider dogs nuisances and will shoot them on sight. (In some communities they hold an annual dog shoot.)

Nicole was immediately attracted to the dog in question. Her name was Maggie, and she resembled a wheaten terrier. About two years old, Maggie had a "face filled with character even though her hair was all shaggy and sticking out all over her body. She looked like a cartoon dog from a Disney movie," Nicole says. But when they first met, Maggie came right up to Nicole and put her front legs around her, as if she was hugging her. That cinched it.

It wasn't easy in the beginning. Maggie snapped at everyone else; she was not socialized around people. Then, the first time she could, she dashed out the door and ran down the street. A neighbor attempted to stop her. Maggie tried to bite her. Nicole was finally able to approach the dog and had to carry her home . . . all forty pounds of her. Nicole and her husband then took Maggie to obedience school so that she could learn basic commands. They discovered that Maggie was a very smart dog who caught on fast.

Since then, Maggie has been slowly acclimating to the life of a beloved house dog.

Six months after the adoption, Nicole noticed that Maggie had a lump in her belly by her leg. Nicole feared it could be a hernia, or worse, and took Maggie to the vet. It turned out to be a BB pellet—someone had been shooting at her at the garbage dump where she'd been found. This certainly helped Nicole understand why it took so long for Maggie to trust other humans.

The vet recommended Nicole leave the pellet in Maggie's body; it would be too invasive a surgery to get it out unless Nicole thought it was bothering the dog. So Maggie retains a memento of her years at the dump. In the meantime she spends her days being petted and loved and chasing Maisie, the cat—not that the cat dislikes it. Maisie will walk through the living room and if Maggie doesn't chase her, she'll walk back and forth until she finally gets the dog's attention, at which point the game is on.

Two Basic Commands: "Sit" and "Stay"

If you've decided you'd like to train your dog in some basic commands by yourself, you can start with the basics: "sit" and "stay." The concepts behind the numbered instructions on the following pages can be applied to most canine training.

Sit

This simple command helps you and your rescue learn the basic concepts of training—and, of course, teaches your dog to sit on command.

Step 1: Exercise your dog. Burn off some energy. Get your rescue to focus on you. Throw a ball, pull on a rope, or go for a walk.

Step 2: Make sure you're in a controlled environment without distractions. Your dog should be focused on you only, and you should be focused only on your dog.

Step 3: With an ample supply of small treats at hand, such as pieces of kibble, some peanut butter, or broken-up treats, take one treat in your hand and hold it in front of your dog about a foot over his head. If he moves forward, raise the treat higher. If he jumps up, wait for him to go back down and then slowly move the treat forward again, still over his head. Your dog will want to sit down to be able to raise his head, at which point you should immediately give him a treat and verbal praise. Repeat this step five to ten times or until your dog is consistently sitting when you move the treat over his head.

Step 4: Keep repeating step three, but now, each time your dog sits, simultaneously say the word *sit* and give your dog a treat. Repeat this step five to ten times as well.

Step 5: Without moving a treat forward, say just the word *sit*. If your dog doesn't sit, repeat step four several more times and then try this step again. Always give treats and praise every time your dog sits. Once your dog has responded only to the verbal command, repeat the process several more times and give your dog plenty of praise.

Step 6: Give the "sit" command randomly throughout the day and when out on walks. This critical part of training teaches your dog to remember she should obey the new command in other locations, and that treats and praise are always at hand for obeying.

Step 7: Begin adding in distractions. If your dog is primarily bothered by other dogs, you may want to start by adding another person to your training session.

When you can get your dog to sit, give him a treat. Once he is sitting and focusing on you regularly, you can then try the "sit" command when other dogs are nearby (but not within reach of your dog). Standing near, but outside, a dog park works well. Going for a walk where your dog can see other dogs can also work, but not if the other dogs are barking and acting aggressively.

Eventually you can work your way up to bringing your dog closer to other dogs. If he becomes too anxious and distracted, return to the normal training routine for a few sessions and work your way back up. Remember that your dog is learning to respond to your instructions and to please you by giving a desired response.

Continue the training often: Try to arrange at least a couple of sessions a day lasting from a few to twenty minutes, depending on how well your dog is responding. Be sure to include exercise and play before training and to be involved with your dog's playtime. Training for a desired response can take a week or a few months, depending on the dog and how often you can provide training.

Stay

"Stay" is a natural progression from "sit." The idea is to teach your dog to settle in one place momentarily. This command does not calm your dog down; it simply buys you time to get a leash on her or prevents her from bolting out the door as you go through it. Your body language, facial expressions, and tone of voice can help calm your dog.

Step 1: You guessed it! Exercise! Burn off your dog's physical energy so she can focus her mental energy.

Step 2: Make sure you are in a controlled environment free of distractions.

Step 3: Use the "sit" command to get your dog to sit down. Then, before giving a reward, hesitate briefly before saying the word *stay* and then immediately give a treat or plenty of praise. This is an excellent time to practice putting both arms around your rescue or grabbing her collar, training her to be calm when you want her to stay in place and not run away. Repeat this step five to ten times or as long as necessary to ensure your dog is consistently sitting in one place without bolting up afterward.

Step 4: Continue to repeat step three, but now wait longer. Try waiting for just a second after you say "stay." Repeat this step two or three times, and then try it waiting for a couple of seconds. Eventually, you can work your way up to longer periods of time, which should really only be a few seconds, since that's the amount of time it takes to put a leash on your dog or walk up to your dog to get her.

Step 5: Begin creating distance between you and your dog, closing that distance, and then giving her a treat. Just as in step four, start small and work your way up to something bigger. Give the "sit" command, then the "stay" command, take a half step back, and then move toward your dog and give her a treat. Repeat this as necessary until your rescue is not lifting herself up off the ground or looking anxious. Eventually, move to taking a full step backward, then several steps, then around a corner, and then briefly out of sight.

Step 6: Begin giving the "stay" command randomly. You know your rescue is getting it when she sits and stays focused on you, anticipating the next command.

Step 7: Begin adding in distractions exactly as explained for "sit."

Other Commands

Once your dog has caught on to "sit" and "stay," you can try training her in more specific behaviors. You can also add in specific training for *when* you want your dog to sit. Just as with "sit" and "stay" training, proceed in small steps.

Let's say you don't want your dog to go charging out the door when you open it. Give the "sit" and "stay" commands, walk toward a door, briefly put your hand on the knob while looking at your dog, and then go back to your dog to give her a reward. After doing this a few times, start looking away from your dog while holding the knob. Next, open the door before returning to your dog for her reward and then go through the door for a brief second. Eventually you can practice going through and closing the door before returning to give a reward.

Using the concepts behind this training method, you can also teach your rescue not to bark when someone knocks on the door (or rings the bell). Start by knocking on the door from the inside while looking at your rescue. Next, open the door, go outside, and knock on the open door. Next, knock when the door is closed and then have someone else knock while you sit or stand with your rescue. This will teach your dog to focus on you, who is holding treats nearby, rather than the sound at the door.

Next, try having someone knock on the door while your rescue stays in place and you are in another room. Finally, be ready to give a big treat when someone randomly knocks on the door for an actual visit and your dog just looks at you instead of staring at the door. Just as in the earlier examples, work slowly, give treats and praise for desired behavior, and have regular training sessions until your dog is consistently staying calm when someone knocks at the door.

If your dog barks whenever she sees someone outside and not just when they knock on the door, you can expand the training to have your dog sit and stay as you stand in view of your dog through a window after shutting the door behind you. You can then work up to standing farther away and then by having a friend accompany you as you stand outside watching your dog as she waits behind a window. Eventually, you can have your friend stand alone and then have someone else come by during the training. If you take it step by step, giving immediate rewards for the desired behavior of waiting quietly—even if only for a moment—your dog will respond to the training.

Doug and Nicky

Nicky, a black-and-white mostly pit bull, hadn't seen his friend Doug Halsey in six years. But Nicky remembered Doug well—wagging his tail wildly and his mouth open, panting with excitement. That might seem a normal response for a happy dog, but without Doug's efforts, Nicky may not have even been able to open his mouth at all.

Many years ago, Doug, working as a volunteer for the rescue nonprofit A Cause for Paws, received an email from the New York City public shelter about a dog who had been found tied up on a Bronx rooftop. "I could see something seemed off—his face was all askew," says Doug. It turned out Nicky had been hit in the face with a blunt instrument that broke his jaw and fused it shut. "When I first met him," Doug says, "all he could do was stick his tongue out, lap up water, and lick up little pieces of dry food."

After rescuing Nicky from the shelter, Doug placed him in a foster home. Nicky's condition stymied several vets, so it was clear he needed to see a specialist. After the initial consultation, the surgeon was not hopeful. But he agreed to give it a shot. Doug then contacted the office of the Mayor's Alliance for NYC's Animals to see if Nicky qualified for financial assistance from the group's medical fund. Nicky did, and was sent to NYC Veterinary Specialists for surgery.

The surgeon had to perform the complex procedure of cutting out a section of Nicky's cheekbone and then connecting his jaw. It was a long shot, but amazingly, the surgery worked. "I visited him in the hospital and when he yawned with an open mouth, I started to cry," Doug says. "It was one of my happiest moments in rescue."

Now it was time to find Nicky a permanent home. Enter Cathie Xenaxis into the picture. The Xenaxis family had been looking for another German shepherd as a companion for their dog, Abby, but after meeting Nicky with his incredible personality, playful demeanor, and incredible story, they were sold. Just as important, so was Abby. Soon Nicky joined the Xenaxis household, and Nicky and Abby became fast friends—playing constantly, snuggling together at night.

Now, whenever Doug visits, Nicky remembers his savior, jumping on him and opening his mouth as if delighted to show off his new jaw. Nor did Doug ever forget Nicky, whose situation impacted him so much that in 2009 Doug founded Ready for Rescue, a New York–based organization specializing in rehabilitating injured and sick animals. To this day, Doug has saved more than 1,300 animals from the streets and shelters of New York City. Ready for Rescue is 100 percent volunteer-run and specializes in senior, sick, or injured animals who have the hardest time making it out of the city shelter.

All the information in this section may seem overwhelming when you're considering adding a dog to your family. Don't worry. The vast majority of rescue dogs adjust to being at a new home with few or no problems. In fact, behavioral or separation anxiety issues often turn out to be nothing more than the normal adjustment phase when a new dog and guardian first live together. No matter what happens, knowing that you've saved a life makes the entire adoption process worthwhile. You may not get exactly what you were expecting from a rescue dog—no more than you can from any relationship—but I guarantee that what you will get are many years of love, companionship, and wonderful memories.

PART III

HELPING
RESCUES
BEYOND
YOUR HOME

JOINING THE RESCUE COMMUNITY

Adopting and fostering dogs aren't the only ways you can help them. There is much that can be done outside of your home to help dogs directly and indirectly as part of the "rescue community."

This rescue community refers to groups of people helping local shelters; aiding in the placement of stray dogs; joining the international effort to save dogs of all kinds, such as donating money to help strays in Europe or rescuing dogs in the dog meat trade in Asia; making strategic decisions about purchasing choices; or becoming an activist in the political arena. The bottom line for the rescue community: Help dogs whenever and wherever there is a need.

For example, my friend Akbar Ali is an actor and writer in Los Angeles, California. Akbar has two dogs and can't adopt any more into his small apartment. Instead, he helps the rescue community by keeping an eye out on social media for posts about dogs at shelters who are old or who have health problems and need to be adopted or they'll be euthanized. These dogs are then picked up and helped by others who have the time and the space.

Here are the three principle ways you can join this world:

1. As a shelter volunteer, you can be an active participant, donating your time, energy, and love.
2. As a conscious consumer, you can avoid products that are tested on dogs.
3. As an activist, you can protest abuses of dogs in many forms. You can also support legislation that offers critical protections for dogs, changing the entire landscape of the fight for our loyal companions.

Become a Volunteer

Volunteering at shelters is one of the best ways to help out dogs and benefit your local rescue community—and have a truly enjoyable time in the process: Volunteering offers opportunities you will never forget. When I have a day off from working undercover and am feeling overly stressed, I often visit animal shelters. As long as the shelter isn't crowded (so as not to keep a dog from a potential adopter), I walk a dog or two around the grounds and hang out in a playpen. It always feels wonderful to love an animal, to throw a ball around for an energetic mutt, to watch a tail wag joyfully while playing tug-of-war with a rope toy.

Most shelters would collapse without volunteers. However, they all operate differently. Some shelters will take you in and put you to work right away, while others have orientation events you must attend before being placed on a volunteering schedule. Some have specific duties they need performed; others are more flexible. Not all volunteer duties are necessarily fun. Poop happens, and somebody's got to clean it up—and there are a lot of other dirty, important chores, including washing dishes and dog toys, doing laundry, mowing lawns, and mopping floors. There are other, more enjoyable chores as well. Most of all, volunteers help shelters by spending as much time as possible with dogs. Unlike commercial dog breeders, good shelters make the psychological well-being of their animals their top priority; this reduces returns by keeping dogs socialized and always ready for a forever home. Walking dogs and setting up play groups is critical to help dogs get out of their enclosures and burn off energy, which makes them calmer around potential adopters. Dogs who seem either too fearful or too hyper are less likely to get adopted. Dogs also need to be regularly bathed and groomed so they look as good as possible for potential adopters.

Training dogs in shelters to understand basic commands (e.g., "sit," "stay," "come," and "heel") is also an important task, not only for the dogs' mental enrichment but also so the dogs can learn how to read a person's instructions and obey them for a reward. If dogs understand this at the shelter, the concept can be transferred over for additional training by an adopter.

For example, the Animal Rescue Fund of the Hamptons (ARF), located in East Hampton, New York, is a no-kill shelter that takes in rescue dogs from all over the world. ARF helps rescue dogs when there's no space for them at other shelters, or when they have no other chance. Dogs from as far away as Puerto Rico and even China have found their way to the Hamptons and into the loving arms of shelter staff and volunteers. ARF takes in about 1,500 animals a year, and volunteers play an integral role in helping those animals feel comfortable at the shelter, making sure they are socialized and prepared for lives in forever homes.

ARF's executive director, Scott Howe, explains that volunteers help establish trust with rescued dogs, sometimes helping the ones who are most fearful and in need of love. Only about 1 percent of the animals that ARF receives are cases requiring an intense amount of behavioral therapy. And that 1 percent of dogs are not "bad dogs" who have somehow failed their owners. It's the other way around. As Scott points out, "Somewhere along the way, people have failed them miserably and so they have lost trust in the world." ARF consistently succeeds in rehabilitating such dogs.

The other 99 percent of dogs who come into ARF simply need love and attention. "It's not just about space and food, it's about socialization," Scott says. "We want dogs to go home and be companions for people, so they need meaningful contact with people every day. To do that, we rely on volunteers for reinforcing positive behavior, training, and assisting staff in rehabilitating dogs with behavioral issues." Volunteering is also good training for you! If you don't know much about dogs, spending time at a shelter and learning training techniques is a great way to gain knowledge of canine behavior before you adopt.

Of course, the easiest step to take as a volunteer is to donate money. Some shelters create fund-raising events such as walkathons, calendars with pictures of their rescues, or social media posts used to sponsor specific rescues who need care—fund-raising is often achieved simply by spreading the word on social media that a shelter needs help.

If you don't want to volunteer for a fund-raising event at a shelter, you can get creative on your own. I've raised funds for shelters when I was selling personal belongings: I reached out to all my friends online and told them the prices I wanted for various items. However, instead of asking for them to pay me in cash, I asked them to send the money as a donation to a local shelter.

You can also help out at adoption events. Many shelters will hold these events in public, or at stores such as Petco and PetSmart. Adoption events help introduce people to rescues when they may otherwise may never visit a shelter. Many rescue groups that are entirely foster-home based require these sorts of events to adopt out their animals, since they don't have a central shelter for the public to visit.

Such events require volunteers. Permits may be needed to stage the event on city property, while dogs, crates, and all supplies have to be ferried between the shelters and adoption sites. Potential adopters will need someone to talk to about adopting rescues. Dogs will have to go on bathroom breaks and be walked. Watching a dog trot off to a permanent home is a rich reward for volunteers, and likely to happen at every adoption event.

Some volunteers become creative with their efforts, using unconventional means to save lives. In Chicago, a nonprofit group called Chicagoland Rescue Intervention and Support Program (CRISP) helps save dogs in the city. CRISP is not a shelter and won't take your dogs. It will, however, help you figure out how to afford vet bills if they become too costly. CRISP will also pay for your dog's training, day care, or for a dog walker. They'll help you deal with your landlord who wants to kick you out for having a pit bull. They'll help you keep your dog if you're moving. And, if you absolutely can't make it work, CRISP will work with no-kill shelters and rescue groups to find your dog a new home. As Sarah Lauch, a volunteer with CRISP, points out, "Our number-one goal is to keep the owner with the animal. No matter what."

Sarah works with a lot of dedicated volunteers who, despite their full-time jobs, find time to volunteer with CRISP to help out in their lifesaving efforts. Sarah is an executive producer for NBC Sports Chicago; other volunteers include a physical therapist for animals, a vice president of operations and property management, a manager for the Big Ten college sports network, and an emergency medical technician. Since CRISP was founded in May 2016, they have prevented more than two thousand dogs from being sent into animal control, where they could be euthanized.

Petfinder has a list of many US shelters and rescue groups that can easily be searched via their database at: petfinder.com/animal-shelters-and-rescues/search/

Become a Conscious Consumer

While the majority of animals used in product tests are mice and rats, dogs are also used for various experiments, including, strangely, testing dog food: Many dog food brands test their food on dogs in laboratories. And although there are protocols that require some form of oversight, not all companies follow them. For instance, recommendations for the food trials state that only 25 percent of dogs can be removed for poor food intake, meaning additional dogs suffering from malnourishment could be forced to stay in the studies.

Unfortunately, the list of dog food brands that do and don't test their products on dogs is ever changing. Dogs are tested through trials in which they are fed and weighed over several weeks. I've worked at enough government-licensed and -inspected facilities that use dogs to know they cannot be trusted to honor their word or follow the law.

To find out more, contact companies directly through research done by the New England Anti-Vivisection Society (NEAVS). NEAVS works to uncover cruel practices in animal testing and works toward alternatives to using innocent animals in experimentation. Here's their list of dog food companies that tested on dogs in 2017: Big Heart Pet Brands, Hill's Pet Nutrition Center, Pet Food Solutions Inc., Nestlé Purina Global Resources Inc., Marshall Farms Group Ltd., and Royal Canin USA Inc.

Countless other products are tested on animals. It's not easy determining which ones use dogs. Research by the Humane Society of the United States (HSUS) reveals that in 2015, 67,181 dogs were used in research, mostly in private laboratories. The largest percentage of grants for dogs were used in cancer, cardiac, neurology, and infectious disease research. For the most part this kind of research is fading because scientists can now grow human cell cultures, as well as human beating hearts, in laboratories. Scientists can even grow miniature human organs for testing using 3-D printers.

To make sure you aren't using products tested on animals, you can visit leapingbunny.org to find cruelty-free products for you and your rescue.

Become an Activist

Join the fight any way you possibly can, even without leaving home—or going far from it. For example, you can help support legislation to fight puppy mills. You can inform dog lovers about why they shouldn't buy puppies from pet stores. You can protest abuses of dogs. You can urge companies to stop using dogs for product testing. This is called being an activist.

Don't let that term make you think you'll be screaming at random strangers who are walking into pet stores. In fact, that's what you should never do. (I've often wanted to confront people walking into pet stores, but I've always stayed respectful, even during protests.) You also don't have to commit acts of civil disobedience. (Although you can if you want to; before I was an investigator, I once handcuffed myself to the door of a Neiman Marcus in Houston, Texas, to protest the store selling fur. That did *not* make the police officers arresting me very happy.) For the rest of you, activism involves simply getting in-person or online petitions signed, attending protests, and helping out with leafletting events. Whether online or in person, a good activist is measured, thoughtful, and well educated about the issue at hand.

For example, Ida McCarthy is CAPS's Illinois state director. She describes herself as "your average retired, married woman." But she doesn't spend her spare time merely relaxing. She regularly organizes protests against pet stores that sell puppies and exposes them for buying from puppy mills. A dauntless woman, Ida organized daily protests for 155 days straight to shut down one such pet store in Lisle, Illinois.

Being an activist means working for a cause. It doesn't mean being a fundamentalist. You don't have to agree with everything I've said in this book to support your local shelter or rescue a stray dog. You don't have to agree with all aspects of the animal protection movement to become involved in it, such as wanting better conditions for dogs at commercial breeding kennels or for pet stores to stop selling puppies from puppy mills. Keep in mind that other activists on your team don't have to be fundamentalists and agree with everything you believe, either. The amazing thing about the movement to protect dogs is that it can include different people from many walks of life. It shouldn't be a polarizing subject.

When the target of my first undercover investigation, Martin Creek Kennels, was shut down and hundreds of dogs were taken by the government, rescue groups across the country were needed to help out. The fact that the kennel was abusing its animals and selling stolen pets to research labs shattered most political divides. Many no-kill shelters made efforts to rescue the dogs, but so did hunting groups, since most of the dogs were traditional hunting breeds such as beagles, Walkers, and blueticks. Although I was working for a vegan activist group that opposed hunting, we were delighted to work with hunting groups to place dogs in homes. The welfare of dogs supersedes politics. Let your activism reflect that. It's about the dogs!

Legislative Activism

One of the most effective types of activism is legislative activism— that is, supporting the creation of laws aimed at ending the abuses of dogs. These laws come in all shapes and sizes. Some laws are outright bans; others are further regulations on already existing industries. Both play important roles. Regulatory laws, such as the welfare laws passed in 2008 in Pennsylvania, may not have outlawed puppy mills, but they cut down on their numbers and improved dogs' living conditions. Bans, on the other hand, completely outlaw something, such as what California did in 2018 by banning all pet stores from selling puppies from breeders. Bans are the gold standard, but they usually come only after momentum has built from previous regulatory laws or, in the case of California, bans that had already passed in major cities.

The lesson here is that we often can't get everything we want in one law. While I would like to see commercial kennels banned altogether, regulatory welfare laws that improve the conditions of puppy mills, even if they are allowed to keep operating, are a step forward.

How to Work on Legislation

If you want to support legislative change, first and foremost make sure you're well-informed. Research the issue carefully and check the sources offering the information. For example, if a piece of legislation is being proposed, find out who supports it and who opposes it. If it's been proposed in the past and failed, find out why. This will help you answer questions the public will have when you discuss the new bill. It will also help you discover where your political representatives stand. Most likely, reputable animal rights groups are aware of all these legislative efforts and can provide you with this information. Staying informed is the foundation of effectiveness. Your head weighs more than your heart, and your knowledge is at least as important as your passion. If your heart tells you to go somewhere, make sure your head steers you along the way.

If you want legislative change, let your representatives know. Send emails and make calls to voice your opinion. Don't be afraid to ask your representatives about their stances on the issues. Be prepared for pushback and deflection, even from politicians you otherwise support. If a politician disagrees with you, make sure you explain that, as a constituent, your views are not being represented. Be specific about why you want more protection for dogs. Animal issues often slip under the radar of public attention. If a politician votes against a bill regulating, say, stricter standards for commercial kennels, many voters won't notice. Make sure your representatives know that you and others are watching. Unlike other issues, it's very difficult to be publicly against helping dogs.

Other forms of action include writing letters to the editor of your local newspaper, reaching out to the public on social media, and joining public demonstrations (see page 230). You can also engage the public one-on-one. Some states allow laws to be passed through ballot initiatives. In these cases, getting petitions signed for the new law is a must. Other times, it's useful to pass out leaflets to the public to inform them of the changes you want to make. If you decide to participate in either of these areas, you must thoroughly understand the issues you're representing, and you must represent them correctly. Always look presentable and act nonconfrontational—even when people are trying to provoke you.

Preemption Laws

Regulations on puppy mills are critical to protecting dogs. Activists must work constantly to make sure these regulations become laws, and also work to make sure they're not overturned. In addition, a major threat to legislation protecting dogs is what's known as preemption laws. In the dog protection movement, this means statewide laws that forbid cities from passing their own bans on pet stores selling puppies from breeders. In other words, if the state government allows it, then all cities and towns must allow it, too.

COURTESY OF THE COMPANION ANIMAL PROTECTION SOCIETY

A puppy sits on filthy cage wire of a USDA-licensed and -inspected puppy mill in Bloomfield, Iowa.

For instance, Petland supports preemption laws so that their stores in densely populated areas can't be prevented from selling puppy mill puppies. The only option activists have is to pass a state law banning all stores from selling puppies from breeders. Obviously, in states with a majority of legislators sympathetic to preemption bills, passing animal rights legislation is next to impossible. In this case, the only hope dogs have are activists willing to educate the public into demanding change from their representatives.

Street Activism

For some people, writing letters and signing petitions isn't enough. You want action! There's a place in the rescue community for you, too. I'm proud to say I was a street activist before I was an investigator. I've been involved in many demonstrations. I've organized countless protests. I've participated in the silent kind, the provocative kind, the productive kind, and the unproductive kind.

A productive protest results in increased public awareness. Protests can reach your target audience directly, such as customers at a pet store that sells puppies from puppy mills. Protests can also generate press coverage, further increasing awareness of your cause. CAPS, which has protested pet stores in numerous states, is an excellent role model. Participants either hold signs and hand out literature in front of stores after obtaining any necessary permits, or walk in front of pet stores at malls. Since malls usually forbid signage, protestors write their anti–pet store slogans on shopping bags. CAPS protestors are always respectful, never confrontational. Protestors can also participate in demonstrations against laws that harm animal welfare, such as dog racing tracks or companies that use dogs for experimentation.

If you're nervous about your first protest, that's perfectly fine. Venture outside your comfort zone. Few people ever actually participate in a protest; it's something "other people" do. Protests bring with them concerns about confrontation. What if someone has tough questions for you? What if someone is impolite? What if someone from the pet store harasses you? Don't worry. Be honest, be polite, and be brave. While protests often involve standing still as people rush past avoiding eye contact, it can also involve engaging in conversations with total strangers. How many of us do that? How often do you leave your comfort zone to talk to someone about an important issue?

When preparing for a protest, make sure you team up with an animal rights group that has organized successful protests and can walk you through the process. Once you see how it's done, you'll realize it's easier than you think. You'll want to understand some basic principles for participating in a protest, know what you'll need to bring, and know the best places to target. Let's start with the basics.

First, make sure you can legally protest where and how you want, and that you have any necessary permits if you want to use equipment such as a bullhorn. A police nonemergency number or city information number (such as 311) can point you in the right direction. Protesting is protected by the First Amendment, but remember that your right to protest shouldn't interfere with someone else's right to walk down the sidewalk, eat in peace, or run their business that happens to be next door.

Second, be respectful to law enforcement. This doesn't mean you must obey commands from a police officer telling you to leave an area in which you have a legal right to protest. I know what it's like to have a police officer screaming in my face as I politely explain that I have a permit to protest. But the vast majority of officers are not like this. Always show respect to them. They're simply doing their jobs. If you are violating your permit, obey the law and move. If the police have questions for you, be courteous and answer them. Make it known you are not trying to make their jobs difficult. The police are protecting you, too.

Third, notify the press. An animal rights group can help you create a press release, tell you how and when to release it, and share its contacts with the media outlets most likely to cover your protest.

Fourth, dress for the part. You want passersby to be able to connect with you. This is not the time to wear an outrageous T-shirt or let the world know your political bent because of the statement on your hat. Be a calm, respectful voice for animals by looking relatable to as many people as possible.

Fifth, bring your A game. Remain in a good mood, be polite to everyone, and be ready to brush off any negative comments thrown your way. I remember my time protesting fur stores in Houston, Texas, with the Houston Animal Rights Team. I was passing out leaflets about fur farms, and I quickly noticed that if a single person in a crowd took one, everyone with them did as well. If that first person turned it down, so did the others. I realized two things: I had to select a person who was most likely to take the leaflet, and I had to look as friendly as I possibly could. Who is making eye contact with you? Who is listening to what you are saying?

Also, remember that one-on-one interactions with consumers are important, but so is media representation. Don't get into a shouting match with that one person who wants to wildly provoke you when the cameras are rolling.

A Final Word

Dogs have no way to complain about their abuse. They can't name their tormentors, talk about their feelings, or list their grievances. We do that for them.

I've been fighting to help dogs for a long time, following the footsteps of extraordinary investigators such as Bob Baker and Gail Eisnitz. Baker was one of the first to investigate puppy mills, and Eisnitz not only uncovered horrible abuses at slaughterhouses but wrote an inspiring book on the subject: *Slaughterhouse: The Shocking Story of Greed, Neglect, and Inhumane Treatment Inside the U.S. Meat Industry.* Despite all the investigations uncovering animal abuse, despite all the new laws to protect animals, and despite all the efforts by animal rights groups to protect dogs, it's not enough. Dogs are still trapped in cages like livestock. Dogs are still used as test subjects for pesticide poisoning. They are forced to fight one another, they are bred for appearance and not companionship, and they are euthanized at shelters because not enough people are adopting them.

Dogs need your help. If you've read this book, and you feel moved, go to work! If you want to see more, do your own research. You can look at the video footage and read the field notes for many of my cases online on the Companion Animal Protection Society website. You can look up the Animal Welfare Act used to regulate USDA-licensed puppy mills and see exactly what it says, then compare that to the video evidence I've obtained. You can go to the Humane Society of the United States' Horrible Hundred webpage, which maintains an updated list of the worst puppy mills in America. You can look at the statistics of how many dogs are euthanized at shelters and see for yourself the hundreds of thousands of lives that need to be saved every year.

You have the opportunity to make a difference by adopting, fostering, or giving special attention to a rescue dog at a shelter. You have the opportunity to take on a local or national cause by donating money, signing petitions, organizing protests, and educating the public. Never underestimate your power as an individual. For a single dog at a shelter, one person can make all the difference in the world. Regardless of who you are, where you live, or what your limitations may be, there's always a way to help dogs. This battle is a team effort. Every member of the team is critical, and every member makes a difference.

My own particular role is to gather evidence, but the team I've joined also includes activists who use that evidence for public education, corporate policy change, and legislative change. It includes prosecutors and law enforcement officers who bust animal abusers, animal rescuers who take animals from abusers to shelters, and all the workers and volunteers who care for the animals at those shelters. The team also includes every member of the public who stands up against animal abuse by donating to animal rights groups, signs petitions to end cruelty to dogs, and chooses to adopt dogs instead of buying puppies from breeders.

I hope the team now includes you. Welcome to the team.

Acknowledgments

Foremost, I thank my parents, who through the years, no matter how difficult and dark, gave me guidance and moral support. They always explained to me the philosophical reasons for doing what is right. I would also like to thank my loving girlfriend, Josie, and our dog, Floyd, for being on my team for this book as well as on our mission to make the world a better place for animals.

I am very grateful for all my friends and colleagues who have helped me in the field or given support out of the field. For security reasons most of them can't be named, but the work they have done and friendship they've offered have been essential. Without Steven Garrett, I never would have made it through my first case. I am eternally grateful to pioneering investigator Bob Baker for his constant guidance in investigating puppy mills. My gratitude and respect go to the Companion Animal Protection Society (which has been more of a partner to me than client), the Animal Rescue League of Iowa, Austin Pets Alive!, the Animal Rescue Fund of the Hamptons (for sharing knowledge of their lifesaving shelters), the Otter Tail County Sheriff's Office and Attorney's Office (for taking down puppy miller Kathy Bauck), the US Attorneys Office of the Eastern District of

Arkansas (for busting the notorious CC and Patsy Baird), and Marsha Perelman (for taking matters into her own hands when puppy mill dogs needed her help). In fact, I would like to thank every animal activist, law enforcement officer, and citizen who has taken a risk, gotten dirty, and helped a dog in need. The world may never know what they've done, and they may have made enemies out of animal abusers in the process, but they are on the right side. I am proud to be on their team.

I am also grateful to HBO documentaries, Nat Geo, Tom Simon of Working Dog Productions, Sarah Teale of Teale-Edwards Productions, my agent John Maas at Park & Fine Literary and Media, and the staff at my publisher TarcherPerigee, especially my terrific editor, Sara Carder, as well as Megan Newman, Rachel Ayotte, Claire Sullivan, Nancy Resnick, Farin Schlussel, Casey Maloney, and Carla Iannone. And, of course, I want to thank my good friends Gene Stone (for helping me put my thoughts into words) and Nick Bromley (for all the wonderful work he has done in turning this idea for a book into an actual book).

Finally, I have to thank Scotty, my childhood dog. Scotty showed me what true companionship, loyalty, empathy, and love look like. May every animal live as long and spoiled as he did.

Index

About the Authors

Pete Paxton (a pseudonym to protect his identity) has been doing undercover animal cruelty investigations since 2001. Widely considered the most prolific investigator in his field, he has investigated puppy mills, pet stores, factory farms, slaughterhouses, and commercial fishing boats, working across the United States and internationally for animal protection nonprofits. Pete has the most thorough experience working undercover at commercial dog kennels of anyone in history; his cases have been the subject of the HBO documentaries *Dealing Dogs* and *Death on a Factory Farm*, both of which won Genesis Awards, and the National Geographic documentary *Animal Undercover*. Pete was awarded the Coin of Excellence from a US Attorneys Office for his first investigation.

Gene Stone, a former Peace Corps volunteer and book, magazine, and newspaper editor, has written, cowritten, or ghostwritten more than forty-five books on a wide variety of subjects, although for the last decade he has concentrated on plant-based diets and their relationship to animal protection, health, and the environment. Among these books are *Forks Over Knives*, *The Engine 2 Diet*, *Mercy for Animals*, *The Awareness*, *Living the Farm Sanctuary Life*, *Eat for the Planet*, and *How Not to Die*.